# A LIFE

*a novel* **WITHOUT**

# REGRETS

Cover design by Okay Creations
Book layout by Lori Colbeck

ISBN-13: 978-1-950348-51-0

# A LIFE WITHOUT REGRETS

a novel

## MARCI BOLDEN

PINK SAND
PRESS

*For Jacob.*
*Now you can see the world from above.*

# ONE

SWEAT BEADED on Carol Denman's brow. The second week of October in Arizona was unbearably hot, but the dry heat wasn't the reason for her discomfort. After signing a waiver, she sat motionless, unable to walk the form to the cheerful brunette who had greeted her for this so-called adventure. Carol's hands had started to shake the moment she'd accepted the clipboard. Ignoring the telltale sign of anxiety, she filled out the blanks and signed away any liability to the company, but she couldn't quite bring herself to hand the paper back to the woman.

Laughter drew Carol's attention to a small group of people she didn't know. Strangers. She was putting her life and safety into the hands of strangers. Everyone except Harold Chu, but she didn't exactly *know* him. She'd met the elderly man the previous afternoon. He was occupying the RV spot next hers at the campground offering the white-water rafting trip she now dreaded. She'd barely parked in

MARCI BOLDEN

her spot before he'd shuffled over and hooked up her RV. Had he been twenty years younger, she would have told him to back off. She was perfectly capable of taking care of herself. However, the kindhearted aura emanating from the man as he chatted like they were old friends soothed her when she may have otherwise been insulted.

They'd made small talk as he connected hoses and plugs, taking much longer than it would have taken Carol to do the job herself. When he was done, he'd smiled and assured her she was all set and then invited her to join him for burgers on his grill. They'd sat at a weatherworn picnic table, sharing stories well after they'd finished eating.

Even so, there were some topics they hadn't discussed. Like how much she was regretting her decision to go on this rafting trip. *Regret* wasn't a strong enough word. The fact was, Carol was terrified. Petrified. Trembling down to her bones. Every shallow, panting inhale she took was a reminder that she was about to climb into an inflatable raft filled with this group of potentially reckless strangers and paddle down the Colorado River. She'd chosen an "adventure" that avoided any of the rougher rapids, but she couldn't avoid getting into a raft. She couldn't avoid the water.

Oh, how she hated the water.

"Howdy, neighbor," Harold said as he eased down next to her on the bench where she sat, clinging to the clipboard like it could save her life. He tipped the bright orange bill of his Orioles baseball cap back on his head and looked her over as if trying to read her thoughts. His silver hair had flecks of black, and wrinkles seamed his face, especially around his eyes and mouth. The lines were evidence of all the warm smiles he'd shared over his lifetime. However, he wasn't smiling as he met her eyes. He appeared concerned. "You feeling okay, Carol?"

She attempted to smile at him, but her lips trembled, so she turned away to focus on a video playing on a large screen. A recording from one of those little cameras that adventurers wore on their helmets showed wild water crashing against a yellow raft, soaking its occupants. "Do you remember I told you I was taking this trip to honor my husband who'd passed away?"

"Yes."

"Well." She tried to swallow, but her throat didn't cooperate. Her mouth was too dry. "Tobias told me so many times that he was going to go white-water rafting someday. He never did, and I recently realized I was the reason. I..." She frowned and gave her head a hard shake as memories from the past sneaked up on her. "I don't like the water. He respected that, but his respect for me deprived him of something he'd wanted to do. So..." Hugging the clipboard to her chest, Carol tore her attention from the screen and back to Harold. "So, I'm going to face my fears and do this for him." Though she tried to sound confident in her decision, her voice trembled.

"You don't seem too excited about that."

Carol had spent years keeping her past in a box on the shelf, doing her best to not let others see how deeply her pain ran. Over the last few months, she'd determined that she had no choice but to acknowledge a lifetime of hurt in order to heal. Even so, the words to explain her fears wouldn't form. "It's more than that... I have some post-traumatic issues that are triggered by water."

Harold stared at her as if he wasn't sure he should share what he was thinking. After a long stretch of silence, he said, "So, you're going to climb into a raft and surround yourself with something you know triggers you? Once you're out on the river, you can't change your mind. They can't turn around and take you back to shore."

Carol bit her lip hard to ward off the lump of emotion mounting in her chest. "I have to face my fears and let them go. I'm tired of holding myself back because I'm scared." The last part came out strained. Admitting that truth hurt. Her fear had stopped her from doing what she knew she should so many times over her lifetime, and she usually thought back with a sense of disappointment in herself. She didn't want to do that anymore. She was trying to heal, and she understood that to do that, she had to learn to overcome her anxieties rather than avoid them.

Harold scanned the group. Eight other people excitedly waited for their adventure to begin. "I don't suppose there's any point in telling you this is a terrible idea?"

Carol smiled somewhat but suspected her effort didn't look sincere. "I have to do this. Not only for Tobias but for myself too."

*And for Katie*, Carol added silently. Her daughter had been gone for twenty-four years, but Carol never failed to consider how Katie would react to things. In this moment, right now, she'd be bouncing up and down, begging Carol to go rafting.

*Please, Mama*, Katie would plead with her tiny hands clasped beneath her chin as she stared up with wide blue eyes. *Pretty please.*

Carol blinked the image of her little girl from her mind before the vision could take hold and bring tears to her eyes.

Harold sat quietly for another long stretch. Though Carol had known him for less than twenty hours, she'd already realized he took time to think before speaking. She liked that about him.

"When was the last time you were in water like this?" he asked.

"I was in the Pacific Ocean over the summer."

"On a boat?"

"No," she answered quietly, her eyes downcast. "I waded out. Only to my knees."

Harold nodded. "How'd that go?"

Carol recalled how she'd panicked. She'd been with Katie's father, John, as they spread their daughter's ashes in the ocean. John had calmed Carol enough to get into the water, but within minutes, her anxiety won out and she'd rushed back to shore. "Not great."

"Do you really think this will be any different?" Harold asked.

"Well, I won't be *in* the water."

Harold gestured lamely toward the video that was still playing. "You're going to get wet, and there's a risk that, even on the milder trips like this one, something could go wrong.

You *could* end up in the water. That's why you have to sign a waiver. Are you okay with that?"

Her heart dropped like a bowling ball carelessly tossed aside. She suspected any remaining color in her cheeks drained as she pictured herself flailing around while the raging river carried her away. Oh, hell. She'd managed to pretend that wasn't a possibility because she'd chosen the trip for beginners. However, falling into the water *was* a possibility. The raft could flip over. She could tumble over the edge. The water could swallow her up. Take her away. *Forever.*

The young woman with the brilliant smile held out her hand as she stopped in front of Carol. "All done?"

Carol furrowed her brow, confused. Her mind was trapped in a loop, imagining the horror-filled screams that would leave her if she found herself drifting away.

Harold pried the clipboard from her fingers and gently squeezed her hand. "Maybe we should do this tomorrow."

An argument formed on Carol's tongue, but she couldn't push the words beyond her lips. She was determined to face her fear. Head-on. Get this over with. Mark white-water rafting off her list of things she wanted to do for Tobias and move forward. All the reasons she wanted to give stuck in her mouth, and she sat there, dumbfounded.

He handed the board to the young lady. "I don't think we're ready yet. We'll come back tomorrow."

"Okay," she said hesitantly before walking away.

Carol let her shoulders sag as a surge of remorse weighed

down on her. "You don't have to stay with me, Harold. You should go with the group."

"We'll come back tomorrow." He stood slowly. Clearly, his age was taking a toll on him, yet he kept going. Hell, he was here for the same reason Carol was. To go white-water rafting. He had to be in his seventies, close to her mother's age, and he was living his life with far more gusto than Carol could, despite her determination to overcome everything holding her back.

"Come on." Harold gestured toward the exit. "There are lots of other things to do around here."

Stuffing her hands into the pockets of her waterproof shorts, Carol wandered out into the sun with her new friend. "I chose this campground because they offered rafting."

"Me too," he said. "They take trips every day but Sunday. We'll come back tomorrow."

Apparently, that was his mantra. The idea sounded nice, but life had proven to her too many times that tomorrow could be snatched away without warning. She was doing her best to get over the habit of putting things off until tomorrow. Tomorrow was not guaranteed.

Katie had been ripped from this life without warning. Carol's father had a heart attack and slipped away before the ambulance had arrived.

And Tobias. He was gone in the blink of an eye.

Carol couldn't count on tomorrow. Tomorrow was *not* guaranteed.

"My son gets that same look when he's beating himself

up," Harold said. "It never helps him feel better. I bet doing so doesn't help you either."

"No," she said. "Not usually. I have this bad habit of hiding from things that scare me." Carol stared at her feet as they started down the dusty path leading them back to the campground. The charcoal gray water shoes she'd bought had never been wet. This was supposed to be their inaugural run. She should have known they'd never make their way into the river when she'd spent almost an hour staring at them on the shelf at the shoe store until she'd convinced herself to buy them. "I'm trying to break that habit," she continued. "I am aware of how much this fear holds me back. If I don't push through this, I'm going to live my life in an endless loop of missing my husband and thinking about what could have been. I'll stop living. Tobias wouldn't want that. I know he wouldn't."

"Mei—my wife," Harold clarified. Carol knew exactly who he'd meant. He'd talked about Mei numerous times the previous evening. "She wanted to travel, but she always made excuses when the time came to actually plan a trip. Finally, one day, I sat her down and told her to close her eyes and point to a place on the map. Wherever her finger landed, we were going."

Carol laughed, picturing Harold and his beloved wife hovering over a map. "How'd that go?"

He shook his head. "She got sick before we could leave. She never made it. We never took that trip."

Carol's smile faltered. "I'm sorry, Harold."

"Cancer," he said. "By the time the doctors caught it, it was too late."

"Tobias was hit by a truck while jogging. The morning was foggy, and the driver didn't see him in time to stop." The words tumbled robotically from her. She'd said them so many times over the last year, they no longer had the ability to steal her breath away. She explained his death as if she were talking about the weather.

Harold let out an audible sigh. "I'm sorry. That's terrible."

She blinked several times, forcing away the image of her husband's broken body lying in a hospital bed. "He loved to travel. That's why I'm on the road right now. I'm trying to honor him. For some reason, I thought he'd want me to go rafting. Maybe I'm..." She let her words trail off as she turned her face up to the clear sky above them. "My mom thinks I'm having a breakdown. Maybe I am."

Once again, Harold was quiet for a stretch before speaking. "I bought that little camper and hit the road last year. My first trip was to the spot Mei had pointed to on the map, this little town in Kansas that we'd never heard of. I didn't stay long. The people were friendly enough, but too many of them noticed me. Minorities find that kind of attention unsettling."

Though Carol was fair-skinned, she understood what he meant. "Tobias was Black. We came across plenty of people over the years who thought they had the right to tell us we didn't belong together."

Harold shook his head. "When I was young, my father

would tell me I'd see changes in my lifetime. I have," he said, "but not as much as I'd hoped."

"The world will get there," Carol said. "I believe that."

"I hope you're right, but the point I was getting to was that I'm here too." He gestured around them at the dusty earth and bright blue sky. "I'm moving on without my wife, like you're moving on without your husband. I don't think you're having a breakdown, Carol. I think you're trying to figure out how to fit into a new and unfamiliar life. That's not an easy thing to do. You're going to miscalculate from time to time."

She smiled weakly at his attempt to support her. Though she appreciated the pep talk, she was still disappointed she hadn't been able to overcome her fears.

When she didn't answer, Harold pressed on. "I have a hard time believing Tobias would want you to put yourself through something that could traumatize you. Do you?"

Carol took a moment to consider what her husband would say to her in this moment. He'd likely say he was proud of her attempt and, like Harold, suggest she try another time. Then, he would have done something goofy to distract her from the depression that crept up on her when she felt she'd failed at something. "Tobias had this way of pushing me *just* hard enough to get me through the tough times. When things get difficult, I retreat into myself and go through life on autopilot. He's gone now. I have to learn how to push myself before I retreat again."

"Maybe this time, you shouldn't push. Maybe this time, you *should* retreat. When I saw you there, I thought you might be sick. You looked like you were close to vomiting."

She chuckled. "I may have been a little anxious."

"A *little*?"

A bird flew overhead, cawing loudly and drawing her attention. "Okay. A lot."

"Maybe Tobias did miss out on something he wanted to do, but you can't make that up to him. I doubt he'd want you to even try if facing this causes you so much stress."

Pressing her teeth into her bottom lip, she tried to use the pain to ward off tears. She'd used that trick a million times in her life, but this was one of the times the emotion overrode the self-inflicted discomfort. "We never had kids," she told Harold. "We tried, but... It was the two of us for so long. He was the center of my world. He was my everything." Her voice cracked, and she swallowed hard. "I wanted to do this for him. He would have loved this."

"How long has he been gone?"

"Thirteen months."

Harold put his hand on her shoulder as they neared the lots where their RVs were parked side by side. "Give yourself more time, Carol. I'm sure there are other things you can do for him. If you want to go rafting, go another time. Not now. You aren't ready."

"I thought we were going back tomorrow," she said as lightly as she could.

He took his hand away. "We can, if you want. I think you should sleep on it, though. We can talk about trying again in the morning. But we can also talk about things you could do for your husband that don't involve water. I bet there were other things Tobias wanted to try that you could do for him."

There were. She'd made a long list, but for some reason, she felt rafting was the most important. Recently, her aunt had accused Carol of torturing herself with her grief. Maybe there was something to that. Carol couldn't deny she tended to be harder on herself than necessary. She could find a thousand things to do for Tobias that didn't cause her to have panic attacks in public. Why had she chosen the one thing that scared her the most?

Because if there was one thing Carol Denman knew how to do, it was finding ways to tear herself down from the inside out. Another habit she had to break.

"Would you like to have dinner again tonight?" she asked her companion so she could stop dwelling on her perceived failure.

Harold smiled, and the concern that had been filling his dark eyes eased. "I'd like that very much. The road gets lonely sometimes, doesn't it? It's nice to make a friend."

"It's wonderful to make a friend. You made dinner last night," she said. "How about if I make a chicken salad? Does that sound good?"

"That sounds great."

She glanced at her watch. "Meet you at the picnic table in two hours?"

"It's a date," Harold said. He climbed the steps into his RV while she climbed the steps into hers.

Once inside, she dropped down into the bench seat at the little table and pressed the heels of her hands into her eyes. A long breath left her as if she'd been holding the spent air forever. What the hell had she been thinking? White-water rafting? Had she lost her mind, like her mom had said?

Turning toward the photo of her and Tobias she'd put on the fridge the day they'd bought this RV, she frowned. "I'm sorry," she said, looking at his smiling face. "I tried."

———

*Carol tugged the blanket tighter around her when she heard Tobias's footfalls on the stairs. If she pretended to be asleep, maybe he'd leave her alone. She needed to be left alone. She loved him for wanting to be there for her, but she needed to be alone.*

*She'd failed him. She'd failed herself. She'd failed everyone.*

*She wasn't ready to face that reality yet.*

*The bedroom door creaked as it opened. He'd been planning to fix that for weeks. His feet rustled over the carpet. Then, the bed sank as he sat on the edge. Carol squeezed her eyes closed. Having him so close made her want to cry again. She'd been crying for days. Her eyes were swollen, and her chest hurt from crying. She didn't want to cry anymore.*

*Tobias rubbed his hand over her back. "Babe," he said softly, "you gotta get up now. You've been in bed for two days."*

*She didn't answer. If she stayed quiet, maybe he'd leave. Instead, he pulled the blankets back and brushed her hair from her face.*

*"I know you're awake, Carol. You're a terrible actress."*

*Forcing her lids over sandpaper eyes, she focused on him. A lump clogged her throat. He looked so sad. He seemed like he was* on the verge of breaking. She'd done that to him. She'd disappointed him so much, she'd broken him.

"I'm sorry," she said. Her lip trembled, and the tears that were constantly too close to the surface fell.

"It's not your fault," Tobias said.

"I should have known something was wrong."

His big shoulders sagged as he shook his head. "You heard the doctor. There's no way you could have known that—"

"Stop," she barked, but her nose was too stuffy to sound as angry as she felt. She didn't need him to tell her what the doctor had said. She'd heard the words over and over in her mind. She heard them in her sleep.

Cervical insufficiency.

That's what the doctor had said. He told her, after two miscarriages, her cervix was too insufficient to carry a pregnancy to term. She'd countered him. She'd had a full-term pregnancy once. She'd given birth once. To Katie.

He said that had been a miracle.

Katie had been a miracle.

The doctor gave them options. There were things they could try, but the risks for another miscarriage were high. Incredibly high. There was no guarantee her body could carry another pregnancy to term. Those words wouldn't stop echoing through her mind. She didn't need her husband to repeat them.

Curling into a ball with her back to Tobias, Carol rested her hand on the stomach that, a few days ago, had a slight bulge where their child had been growing. Tobias hadn't said the words yet, but she knew he would. They wouldn't try again. They wouldn't take the risk, even now that the doctors

14

were aware of her condition and could take preventative measures.

He shifted on the bed behind her. A moment later, he snuggled close, wrapped his arm around her, and put his hand over hers. After kissing her head, he sighed loudly. "You're starting to stink."

Carol didn't want to laugh, but she did, even though the sound was more like a sob. "Screw you," she whispered.

He pulled her closer. "We're in this together. You and me. We're a team, remember? Don't shut me out."

Closing her eyes again, she tried to stop her tears. She couldn't. "This isn't fair to you. This is my punishment, not yours."

He leaned up. "What does that mean? Punishment for what?"

Carol clenched her jaw, not wanting the words to escape her, but she couldn't stop them. "For what happened to Katie."

Grabbing Carol's shoulder, Tobias forced her onto her back and gripped her face. He wasn't hurting her, but he was forceful enough she had no choice but to see the anger in his eyes. "Get that mess out of your head right now," he said sternly. "This has nothing to do with Katie."

"I never should have—"

"Stop it, Carol. I mean it. Katie's death was not your fault. Losing our babies was not your fault. I'm not going to let you think like that."

She knocked his hand away and struggled to sit so he wasn't looming over her, challenging her. Usually when he pushed her, she appreciated the nudge. She was well aware of her ability to get lost inside her head and ignore the problems around her, hoping they'd resolve on their own. But she wasn't going to be pushed this time. She leaned against the stack of pillows she'd burrowed into since coming home from the hospital. Shoving Tobias's shoulder, she glared at him. "Don't you dare tell me what to think."

"Don't you dare make this into something it isn't. Your body can't handle the stress of pregnancy, Carol. That has nothing to do with Katie."

"What kind of mother can't protect her children?"

As soon as the words left her, so did the oxygen in the room. There it was. The guilt she'd been hiding for years. The shame she'd forced down since the day her daughter had died. What kind of mother couldn't protect her child? What kind of mother went against her instincts when she feared for her child's safety?

Carol gasped as the question lingered between them. Hot tears fell unchecked down her cheeks as memories flashed through her mind like a horror film on fast-forward. Katie's smile. Katie's limp body in her arms. Two red rain boots that would never be worn again.

The crib that she and Tobias had bought months ago that would never hold their child.

A sob erupted from Carol before she could stop it. "I can't do this," she managed to say as he yanked her to him. "I can't."

Tobias wrapped her up so tightly, she thought he might be trying to pull her inside him. He kissed her head over and over, holding her like he would never let go, as she wept for the children she'd never held and the child she'd never hold again.

When she finally found her voice again, she whispered, "I'm sorry."

Leaning back enough to see her face, he wiped her cheeks dry. "Don't apologize. I should have realized this would bring up memories of Katie."

"No." Carol swallowed before whispering, "I'm sorry I've disappointed you."

Once again, the air was drawn from the room. Something shifted in Tobias's eyes, and she feared what he was going to say. Maybe he'd been waiting for the right time to tell her didn't want a wife who couldn't give him a family. By admitting her failure, she'd opened the door. He looked like he wanted to walk through it. Or, to be more accurate, out of it.

He stared into her eyes for several seconds before cupping her face. "You have never disappointed me," he stated. "Life isn't fair. This isn't fair. But I'm not disappointed in you. And you haven't let me down. We are going to get through this." After dropping his hands, he let out a slow breath. "I'm going to call Mama. I'm going to have her stay and help us."

"No—"

"I'm scared for you, Carol," he whispered. "I'm scared of what you're doing to yourself. You think I don't see you struggle with Katie's loss more than you want me to know? You think I don't see how you get lost in your own head sometimes? I think... I think we gotta face that. I think we gotta get serious about finding someone to help you."

She furrowed her brow. "No. I don't need help."

"I'm going to ask Mama to stay with us for a while."

"To analyze me?"

17

*He didn't deny her accusation. "To make sure we get through this okay. Both of us." Standing up, he pulled the blankets the rest of the way off the bed. "First, though, let's get you showered and dressed. You'll feel better once you get out of this bed."*

*"Tobias, I'm not..." She stopped talking when he sniffed and wiped a tear from his eye. He was discreet, but she'd seen him, and the movement caused the world to stop. Seeing him shaken gave her grief pause, and for the first time since leaving the hospital, she stopped thinking about* her *pain.*

*He'd lost a child too. Two of them now. The first miscarriage was several months ago. She'd been in her second trimester when the bleeding had started. He'd clung to her hand while he drove her to the emergency room, reassuring her over and over that everything was going to be okay. The second time, she'd been at work when the discomfort started. She'd driven herself to the obstetrician and called Tobias after being admitted to the hospital. The baby was gone before he'd arrived.*

*She'd been spiraling downward since, so much so that she hadn't stopped feeling sorry for herself long enough to consider her husband.*

*God, how could she not have seen how much this had hurt him too?*

*Getting on her knees, Carol crawled to him and wrapped her arms around his neck. "I love you," she said softly.*

*He pulled her against him. "I love you. More than anything."*

*"I'm going to be okay. I promise."*

*"But until you are, I want Mama here to help us."*

*Though Carol didn't want her mother-in-law hovering over her, she nodded. If Tobias wanted his mother there, then Mary should be there. Carol might not be able to give him the children they wanted, but she wouldn't deny him the comfort of having his mother there to help him grieve.*

*"Okay," she whispered and then kissed him. "Okay."*

*Carol was exhausted, but she forced herself off the bed and into the bathroom to shower. For Tobias. As much as she wanted to curl up in a ball and let the world fade away, she had to keep going for Tobias.*

———

Carol knew Harold was right. Beating herself up never did make her feel better, but she was *so* incredibly good at it. She'd learned how to blame herself at a young age and had yet to break the habit despite recognizing how destructive the negative inner talk could be.

Ever since losing Tobias, Carol couldn't seem to escape the depression closing in on her. Sometimes, the sense of loss consumed her. She'd managed to fight her way back each time, but every battle seemed more hard-won than the last. Eventually, she was going to lose. She knew that, and still, she denied the truth as much as possible.

She'd recently promised her mom she'd find a counselor to help her. Being on the road gave her a good excuse not to follow through. How could she commit to therapy if she was traveling? The truth was, she could. She had a phone and a computer. She could find someone to work with her via either of those methods. Finding the courage was another story.

However, she'd been so terror-stricken earlier in the day, she hadn't been able to move. She'd panicked until she could barely function. Ignoring her problems had always been easier for her, but that kind of visceral reaction was not something she could overlook.

This was the point when she had to reach out for the help she clearly needed or accept that she was going to spend the rest of her life avoiding the things that scared her and missing out on adventures Katie and Tobias would have enjoyed. Tobias would tell her to make the call. Send the e-mail. Do whatever she had to do to connect with someone who could guide her to the other side of this hell.

He wouldn't want her to suffer like this. Seeing her like this would break his heart.

She knew that because he'd tried to gently push her into therapy so many times over the course of their marriage. She'd only ever budged one time after the fifteenth anniversary of Katie's passing sent her spiraling into the depths of depression. Carol only went once, though. With faked smiles and nods at the appropriate times, she managed to convince the therapist she was doing as well as could be expected and that Tobias was unnecessarily concerned.

Carol was so well-practiced at hiding her pain, she'd even convinced herself. She put her grief in a box, tied a pretty ribbon around it, and put the package on a shelf, right next to all the other boxes filled with ugliness she couldn't stand to see.

She couldn't seem to find a box big enough to put this pain in, though. Even if she did, there didn't seem to be any room left on the shelf. As much as she hated to admit that her mother was right, Carol couldn't keep denying the toll her sorrow was taking on her. Tobias's loss was the one that had done her in. She was facing her demons alone now, and she was beginning to accept that she couldn't keep them at bay without someone to help her. She couldn't win this fight alone. She had to reach out before she was consumed.

Carol's phone rang, startling her, and she laughed slightly at her reaction. Seeing her mom's name on her caller ID, she debated if she should answer. Considering she was finally accepting that she needed to stop procrastinating and take her mother's advice, Carol wasn't really in the mood to hear the *I told you so* her mom was sure to dish out. However, if she didn't take the call, her mom would worry herself into a fit. Nobody needed to deal with that.

Forcing a smile to her face and hoping the fake happiness translated to her voice, Carol answered. "Hey, Mom."

"What's wrong?" Judith asked immediately.

Letting her shoulders sag, Carol closed her eyes. Clearly, her plan to hide her emotional distress had failed. "Nothing. I had a long day, that's all."

"Why? What happened?"

In the background, Aunt Ellen's voice, muffled by distance from the receiver, came through the line. "What's going on?"

Carol scowled as she imagined the scene playing out on the other end of the phone. Her mom and aunt had lived together for three years now, but Carol couldn't think of two sisters as ill-suited to sharing living quarters as Judith and

Ellen. Where Judith was gruff and direct, Ellen was gentle and coaxing. Ellen would have approached her concerns with tenderness rather than the brash demands Judith had made.

"Mom," Carol said, but she was too late. The bickering between the sisters began.

"I don't know yet," Judith told Ellen with a snappy tone, no doubt shooing at Ellen to leave her alone. "You're talking over me. As you do."

"Mom," Carol called again.

"Let me talk to her," Ellen insisted.

Carol knew what the response would be before Judith could say the words.

As expected, Judith barked, "She's *my* daughter."

Not the least bit deterred, Ellen said, "Put her on speaker." Moments later, Ellen's voice echoed with the telltale signs that Judith had set the call so both women could hear Carol. "Honey, what's wrong?" Her aunt's question was tender, not demanding.

"Nothing's wrong," Carol answered. The silence on the phone let her know they didn't believe her. "I...I tried to do something today that didn't work out. I'm disappointed. That's all."

"What were you doing?" Judith pressed.

Carol debated lying. She didn't want to delve into this with her mom and aunt, but lying was pointless. They'd get the truth from her at some point. "I tried to go on a white-water rafting trip."

More silence.

The women were probably staring at each other through their shock. A hint of amusement found Carol as she pictured them with comically wide eyes and gaping mouths.

"Carol," Ellen finally said, her voice soft and filled with concern.

Then, Judith cut in with her sharp voice. "Why on earth—"

"Mom," Carol said, cutting off the question. "This was something Tobias wanted to do. He always wanted to go rafting, but he never went because of me. I...I wanted to do that for him, but I couldn't. I signed up for the beginner trip because the rapids were supposed to be mild, but...as soon as I imagined the water splashing over me...I froze. I couldn't do it."

"Honey," Ellen said. That was all she said. There was nothing more to add.

Trying to climb into an inflatable raft and navigate down a river had been foolish. Stupid. Impossible.

Tears burned Carol's eyes. "I wanted to do that for him." As much as she'd wanted to pretend that she was okay for her mom and aunt, her voice quivered, betraying the depth of the ache in her soul.

"Carol," Judith said. Though she wasn't affectionate by nature, the way she said her daughter's name could almost pass as warm.

As much effort as the two of them had made in the last few months, going from barely speaking to doing their best to be open and honest, Judith still didn't have the innate ability to offer comfort. That was Ellen's job.

"Listen to me," Judith continued. "It's time to stop this madness and come back to Florida."

"Judith," Ellen chastised.

"No," Carol's mom stated. "We never should have let her leave. You should not be alone right now."

When Carol's last visit to Florida started winding down, Judith had argued every way she could, trying to convince Carol to stay. Finally, she simply frowned and shook her head. While Carol had left on good terms and with much more love in her heart for her mom than she'd ever had before, she hadn't wanted to stay. Judith had a way of making Carol feel less than she was. She now understood her mom didn't make her feel like that intentionally; the woman simply didn't know how to be maternal. After harboring decades of resentment toward her parents, Carol had come to realize they'd done the best they could.

Even so, Judith was never going to be able to offer Carol the support she needed. Carol knew that.

"You need to be in counseling," Judith said, for likely the hundredth time in the last few weeks.

"I'm aware of that," Carol said, finally admitting that she understood how far she'd fallen.

Again, the silence on the line lingered.

"What are you waiting for?" Judith asked.

*Today*. Carol had been waiting for today. She'd been waiting for the moment when she slammed face first into her problems and could no longer deny how all-consuming her grief had become.

"If you don't want to come here," Ellen offered, "go stay with Mary. You know she'd love to have you."

Tobias's mother would indeed love to have Carol there with her. Mary had offered a dozen times as well. The spare bedroom, the one Carol and Tobias used to sleep in, was stacked with boxes from the house Carol had recently sold. Mary had offered to unpack the belongings, but Carol wanted to do that herself. Mary used that as a reason for Carol to come for an extended stay.

"Come home, baby," Mary would tell her every time they spoke. "Come sort out this mess I made in your room."

*Your room*. It was no longer Tobias's room. Now the space was Carol's room. Just Carol's.

Carol swallowed, trying to ward off the tears that had been close to spilling over. "I'll be headed to Mary's soon," she said once she felt strong enough to speak.

"How soon?" Judith asked.

"I'm spending Thanksgiving with Tobias's family. I'll get there a few days early and stay a week or so after. Then, I'll be headed to your place for Christmas." Carol raked her hand through her hair before resting her forehead against her palm. "We've talked about this. Remember?"

Judith sighed. Carol knew the sound came from Judith because dramatic sighs were her mother's signature response. She didn't have to say she thought Carol was being difficult. Her exaggerated exhalation said so.

"We remember," Ellen said. "But we were hoping..."

"You shouldn't be on the road alone," Judith stated, getting to the point her aunt had been about to tiptoe around. "We're worried about you, and we need you to come back."

"I'm okay, Mom."

"No, Carol," her mom countered. "You're not. You're grieving your husband—"

Carol rolled her eyes as she finished for her mother. "In an RV, all alone. I'm aware of that."

Ellen spoke softly. "We really are worried."

"I'm sorry. I don't mean to upset you," Carol said. "I really don't, but—"

It was Judith's turn to finish Carol's statement. "You're working through it."

Carol laughed lightly. "Yeah. I am. I love you both. We'll talk tomorrow."

"She's blowing us off," Judith muttered. "Do you hear that? She's blowing us off."

"Good night, Carol," Ellen said, despite Judith's frustrated tone. "We love you."

"Carol," Judith started. By the way her voice cut off abruptly, Carol guessed Ellen was giving her sister a silent warning. Another sigh, and then Judith said, "I love you. Good night."

"Good night." Carol ended the call and dropped her phone carelessly on the table.

She knew they were worried about her. She understood their concerns. Doing something about what worried them was the hard part. That was the step she hadn't been able to take, the line she hadn't been able to cross. Carol didn't want to spend her life in mourning, and she understood she couldn't find her way out on her own. She knew those things, and she knew what she had to do about them. But the fear of facing the hurt from the past had hold of her, preventing her from doing what she had to. This... This was Tobias's area of expertise.

"Stop being such a chickenshit," she muttered to herself.

Grabbing her laptop, she lifted the top and pressed the power button. As the computer booted up, she opened the notebook she'd used to make extensive notes on every single online therapist her insurance would cover.

Research was one of her favorite ways to procrastinate.

Thinking of Harold and Mei leaning over a map, Carol closed her eyes and pointed at the page where she'd listed several online therapists that fit her criteria. No more delays. No more excuses.

Moving her finger, she read the name she'd selected. *Susan Baxter*. Before she could talk herself out of it, Carol entered the website she'd listed with Dr. Baxter's name and clicked on the option to register as a new client.

# TWO

CAROL HAD BEEN an early riser for years. She and Tobias used to jog every morning before getting ready for work. She wasn't nearly as committed to that routine as she used to be, but she still liked to get up and watch the sun rise as she sipped coffee and ate breakfast. Seeing the sun come up was a good reminder that she was living a new day with new possibilities. A new chance to take the steps she needed to keep going.

One step at a time. That's what Mary told Carol whenever life without Tobias overwhelmed her. She liked her first step of the day to be watching the sun.

She usually sat alone, but when she emerged from her RV, Harold was there to greet her. He smiled brilliantly and toasted her with his mug.

"Howdy, neighbor," he said, as he had since she'd parked her RV next to his.

"Morning."

Sitting across from him at the shared picnic table, Carol watched Harold lift an iced brownie to his mouth. "Is that your breakfast?" she asked.

"It is," he stated, as if eating dessert for breakfast wasn't the least bit strange. "I eat one every morning. If I don't survive the day, at least I got to have one last brownie. Would you like one?" He pushed a second plastic-wrapped treat toward her.

"No, but thank you for offering." She showed him her bowl. "I have oatmeal."

"I could think of a million other things I'd rather eat than oatmeal," he said before taking another bite.

Grinning at the man sitting across from her, Carol could honestly say befriending him, no matter how briefly, was one of the highlights of the past year. She wasn't naive enough to think elderly men couldn't be as dangerous as anyone else. Traveling alone made her a target for anyone with malicious intent. But Harold had been more fatherly than threatening from the moment he'd taken over hooking up her RV without being asked.

One thing Carol had learned when she and Tobias started traveling a few years ago was that fellow wanderers instantly felt comfortable with their temporary neighbors. For the day or so that their paths crossed, strangers became like old friends, sharing stories and watching out for one another. Now that she was traveling alone, those short-lived bonds alternated between lifesavers and paranoia-inducing.

However, with Harold, she was lucky to have met him. He fell into the lifesaver category. She had no doubt he was a good man. An honest man. As they were eating dinner the night before, she'd thanked him more than once for his intervention. Even so, she didn't think he'd ever fully understand how much she appreciated him stopping her before she could climb into a raft. That would have been disastrous.

They sat quietly, eating and drinking coffee as the sky lightened. When she scraped the spoon against the side of the bowl and scooped up the last bite of her oatmeal, he grinned at her.

"How's that taste?" he asked.

"I like oatmeal," she informed him.

"Nobody *likes* oatmeal," he countered with a sly grin and a wink.

She laughed but didn't argue. While oatmeal might not have been her first choice, she'd eaten the dish long enough that she didn't mind the taste or texture. Tobias had been on the college football team when they'd met, and his healthy habits beat out her bad ones. She'd stopped eating junk food decades ago. She wasn't going to backtrack now, especially not with a prepackaged, processed brownie.

"What brought you to Arizona?" Harold asked. "Besides the rafting trip."

"That was it, really," she said. "I wanted to be in the south during winter. I don't like the cold much."

Harold popped the last of his brownie into his mouth and brushed his hands together. "You really sold everything, huh?"

Carol nodded. "I really did."

"Seller's remorse?"

"A little bit," she admitted. "But I was sinking into a depression living in that house alone. There was too much space. Too many memories holding me back."

"But having a home would be nice. Someplace to hang the hat. Someplace to spend the holidays."

Carol set her empty bowl aside. "I'll head to my mother-in-law's house soon. She's in Missouri. I'll be there through Thanksgiving, and then I'm headed to Florida to see my mom."

Carol couldn't believe she'd said that last part without cringing. Three months ago, she and her mother only spoke out of obligation, but they'd taken big strides in mending their relationship in recent months. Now, her mother insisted Carol check in every time she arrived and left a new campground. And she usually texted Carol at least once a day. That meant quite a lot, considering Judith Stewart loathed texting.

Like Harold, Judith couldn't quite understand why her daughter chose to sell almost everything she'd owned to live full-time in an RV. Sometimes, Carol secretly wondered why, too, but she couldn't bring herself to fully admit that she'd started to doubt the decisions she'd made in the last six months. In all honesty, Carol was starting to question every decision she'd made over the past year since she'd been widowed.

She missed her house. Up until she'd sold it, she could pretend that Tobias wasn't gone. She could, somewhere in the back of her mind, tell herself he was on a trip or working late. She could act like her life hadn't been upended. She could sit at the little table in his garden, sipping her wine and reliving the many times she'd watched him tend his flowers.

The downside of that was the heart-stopping recollection she'd have when reality set in and she'd remember Tobias was dead. Not on a trip. Not working late. He was gone, and he'd never come home. He'd never tend to his flowers again.

"Your mind is wandering." Harold tilted his head. Concern returned to his eyes.

Carol grinned as the warmth of embarrassment filled her cheeks. "Sorry. I do that. I've had a way of getting lost in my thoughts for as long as I remember."

"May I ask where you went?"

Crossing her arms, Carol leaned onto the picnic table. "Oh, I was trying to figure out how I got here."

"*Here* being Arizona or this point in your life?"

"This point in my life. How long was Mei gone before you figured out how to be yourself without her?"

Harold shook his head slightly. "I don't know that I am myself yet, to be honest. We spent over fifty years together."

"Tobias and I were married almost twenty years. Went by so quickly."

"And the next twenty years will go by quickly as well." Harold pointed a crooked finger her in direction. "Remember that. You don't want to look back and regret the life you lived. Or didn't live."

Carol frowned. "I've been thinking about that. Too much, probably." The sky above them was changing colors as the sun crested the horizon. Darkness faded into light as if even the universe was trying to make her understand the importance of moving on. "He's only been gone thirteen months. We went through so much together. It's okay if I'm not ready to face things without him. Isn't it?"

"Yes," Harold said. "What's not okay is hanging on to the past like your memories can save you. They can't. You'll get frozen in time."

"I made an appointment with a therapist last night. I think it's time." The words were out her mouth before she even considered she shouldn't say them. She barely knew this man but had confessed something incredibly intimate. She held her breath, waiting for his response.

"That's good," he said. "Having someone to talk to will help."

Releasing the air in her lungs, she realized how scared she'd been that he was going to judge her. What a foolish response. With the hell she'd been through, seeking help was nothing to be ashamed of.

"Even the strongest of us need someone sometimes," Harold said, as if he sensed her relief.

"You sound like my aunt. She's tried to convince me I'm stronger than I think for most of my life."

"Why don't you believe her?"

Taking in the sky above them, Carol shrugged. "I've spent most of my life hiding from the things that scare me."

"We're all scared, kiddo," Harold told her. "Every single one of us is scared of something. But you can't let fear stop you."

"I let fear stop me yesterday."

Harold sipped his coffee. "Still beating yourself up about that?"

"A little."

"Whatever caused you to be terrified of the water wouldn't go away if you went white-water rafting," Harold pointed out. "Nor would putting yourself through that help you make peace with losing your husband."

"Ouch." Carol winced dramatically, causing him to grin.

"I'd apologize, but I wouldn't mean it. You needed to hear that."

"Yeah. I guess I did."

"There's something else you need to hear."

She focused on the sincerity in his dark eyes. She imagined if she spent enough time with Harold, he could help her solve all her problems. She doubted he had that kind to waste on her, though. The list of problems they'd have to solve was long.

"Healing isn't about overcoming your loss, Carol," he said gently. "Healing is about living *despite* your loss. The loss becomes easier to bear because you *are* living, but it never goes away."

After letting his words sink in, she knew they were true. Her lip trembled as she thought about how she'd never stopped missing her daughter but had somehow managed to build a life with Tobias. That pain would find her far too often, but she'd learned to carry on. She would again, given time.

Nodding slightly, Carol blinked before her tears could fall. "I'm trying," she whispered.

"I know," he said gently. "It's hard, but you'll find your way."

Dragging her fingers under her eyes, Carol sniffed. "You don't happen to have a map, do you?"

"No, but I do have this." He reached into the pocket of his faded denim shirt and pulled out a thin, oval-shaped, pink rock. "This was Mei's. I want you to have it."

Carol stared for several seconds, only taking the gift from him when he pushed the stone even closer. She laughed lightly when she flipped the rose quartz over and found No Regrets etched on the other side.

"She had worry stones for everything," Harold explained. "I have an entire box full. Sometimes, when I'm having a hard day, I close my eyes and choose one. Every time, I feel like I'm getting a message from her. Last night, when I was trying to think of how to help you, I remembered how she asked to see this one the day before she passed. She pressed it between our palms and made me promise I wouldn't stop living once she was gone. No regrets. That's a pretty good motto, don't you think?"

The image of Harold and Mei holding the stone between their hands tugged at Carol's heart. If she had that kind of memory with Tobias, she wouldn't want to part with the reminder. Perhaps Harold didn't understand how precious that moment had been because he'd been able to say goodbye to his love, but Carol knew. Tobias had been ripped from her without warning. She hadn't gotten to say goodbye to him. This was more than just a stone. This was a connection to his wife that he shouldn't part with.

"Harold, this is very kind, but—"

"No buts," he said.

"This is precious to you."

"You need this more than I do," Harold insisted. "Mei would say so too. Take it."

Running her thumb over the letters, feeling the ridges against her skin, Carol smiled. The coolness of the quartz was soothing in a way she couldn't explain. "Thank you."

"You've had a lot of bad days since losing Tobias, but you *will* have good ones again. Sooner than you realize. Don't forget that."

"I won't." Carol wrapped her fingers around the rock and squeezed. "I'm really glad that I met you."

"Me too." He put his hand over hers, and she opened her fingers so the stone was pressed between their palms, much like she imagined he and Mei had done. "Learning to live again is hard, but you will find your way. I believe that."

"Thank you, Harold."

Pulling his hand back, he said lightly, as if they hadn't just shared an incredibly intimate moment, "I was planning a hike this morning. Would you like to join me?"

Carol wriggled her toes in her slippers. "Give me a minute to put on real shoes." After carrying her bowl inside, she set the dirty dish in the sink and tucked Mei's worry stone into her pocket so she could pull on her tennis shoes. She grabbed a bottle of water on her way out and met Harold back outside.

"Rose quartz," he said without prompting or explanation as they started toward the nearby trails, "is believed to heal the heart chakra. Whenever you start feeling sad, you grab hold of that worry stone and let it help you through."

Carol grinned as she realized she was unconsciously squeezing the stone in her pocket. "I'll be holding it a lot, won't I?"

"For a while, yes. But you'll find you need that kind of help less and less over time."

Carol listened as Harold shared another story of Mei, how she'd started her collection of worry stones and learned how each one had a special purpose. Harold grinned wistfully as he told Carol how his wife had been a natural healer, a kind spirit, and always gave more than she received.

Carol was happy to listen to his stories. Hearing about Mei helped keep her mind off Tobias. Having a break from her tendency to dwell on the past was nice.

"Now that was worth the hike," Harold said, causing Carol to focus on their surroundings.

The path had led them to a wire railing intended to prevent people from getting too close to the edge. The layers of exposed rock below them reminded Carol of the Grand Canyon but on a much smaller scale. In some ways, that made this chasm more beautiful. Tourists weren't flocking to this view, crowding around as if they were the only ones who mattered. The peace here made the view more special, more astonishing. The quiet of the moment added to the impact. There were no other hikers around, no sounds of people gasping and rushing to see the next wonder.

There was simply peace and a beautiful view that was made for them.

Harold put his arm around Carol's shoulder and pointed up at two sunbeams bursting through several clouds. "Look at that," he whispered, as if not to break the spell. "There they are. Mei and Tobias are smiling down on us. They're happy we met too."

Carol stared at the beams with the same hope that Harold had voiced. Mei and Tobias were there with them.

Maybe Carol hadn't taken the rafting trip she'd planned, but Harold was right. She could feel Tobias there, wrapping her in the love she'd been missing all these months. The sensation hit her out of nowhere, making her choke. The sob that pushed out rippled through the still air. Harold hugged her closer, patted her shoulder, and pulled a tissue from his pocket as she cried.

———

*The quiet of the Colorado morning was hypnotic. Carol had lived in cities all her life. Sirens or car horns were constantly wailing in the background. Though she and Tobias were in a campground, there was so much space. She felt like she was sitting in the wild as the sky brightened before the world woke. The quiet was eerie but peaceful.*

*When they'd decided to run a marathon in Denver, Tobias had this crazy idea to rent an RV and turn what was supposed to be a quick weekend trip into a vacation so they had time to acclimate to the higher altitude. When they went to look at rentals, his little spark of an idea had ended with them purchasing a compact motor home. Though Tobias was always thoughtful in his choices, he was also spontaneous like that. He jumped at chances. Everything was an exciting experience waiting to happen.*

*He was nothing like Carol when it came to taking chances. She was an overthinker. She paused at the edge and peered down, debating how wise jumping would be. Then she calculated the best way to land so she knew what she was in for before her feet ever left the ground.*

*She thought she was getting better, more easygoing, but she doubted she'd ever be as bold as her husband. She'd never feel so comfortable with life so as to fully embrace it. Life had let her down too many times to be so impulsive.*

*Tobias was the bolder of the two. She was the worrier, the planner, the caretaker. While he'd slept like a baby all night, she'd been on high alert, wondering how safe they were inside the vehicle. She'd given up even trying to get any sleep around four in the morning and started a pot of coffee while she dressed. Once she had a cup in hand, she moved to a chair outside the RV as the sky was brightening over the horizon.*

*The sun was peeking at her when she heard the RV door open. Tobias stepped outside and muttered, "There you are," before sinking into the chair next to her.*

*She chuckled as she glanced over at him, realizing he seemed more tired now than when they'd finally crawled into bed the night before. "I was trying to let you sleep."*

*"You know I don't sleep when you're so restless." Though his tone was rife with annoyance, Carol heard the underlying concern in his mumbled words. He sipped from the mug he'd brought with him. "What kept you up all night?"*

*"Paranoia," she confessed with a light voice in contrast to his gruff one. "I spent all night wondering how we would escape if the RV caught on fire or if someone broke in."*

*He laughed wryly. "You're so morbid sometimes."*

*She shrugged, unable to disagree with his observation. "Maybe. But we should add a sturdier lock to the door. Maybe get another extinguisher to keep by the bed."*

*He didn't try to talk her out of either. When she got an idea like that in her head, the easiest way to get rid of the thought was to simply follow through. However, he did say, "I wish your brain had a switch so I could shut your thoughts off once in a while."*

*She laughed as she toasted him with her mug. "You and me both."*

*Quiet fell between them as birds chirped and the world stirred. As the sound grew to include insects, the peace inside her took another one of those darker turns she tended toward. Sometimes, when the world around her got too quiet, the sadness in the back of her mind reached out to her. Her soul had never learned to embrace peace. Peace was unsettling for reasons she'd never understood.*

*Whenever her mind would calm, a whisper would echo through her, reminding her of all the pain she'd lived through, mostly losing Katie. All these years later, she could still be brought to her knees without warning.*

*Tobias tilted his head down and eyed her as if he sensed the shift in her thoughts. She never could hide from him. His superpower was seeing through the facade she'd spent her life* creating. "I hope you aren't imagining us burning to death, Carol. It's too early in the morning for that kind of shit."

Her lips curved up at how disgruntled he sounded. "Actually, I was thinking..." Her smile softened as she voiced what had suddenly clouded her mind. "We're never going to have kids, are we? It's been years since we lost the babies. We've never even talked about what our options were to try to have a family. Now, we're getting too old."

Tobias sipped his coffee, clearly using the act as a way to figure out what to say next. After several long seconds, he put his mug in the other hand so he could reach out and grasp Carol's. "We're not old. Well, I'm not."

Her lips quirked up again. Rather than respond to his reminder that she had a few years on him, she turned her palm up and entwined their fingers. They'd met in college, but while he'd gone straight out of high school, Carol had returned after several years working as a nurse...and being a mother to Katie. "Nice diversion," she said.

Staring out at the mountains, he took his time again. Though he could be spontaneous in some areas, he liked to think before speaking, especially when the topic was as sensitive as children. Talks of children inevitably led Carol to thinking of Katie, which had a way of sinking her into a depression that could last for days. "This is the right life for us," he said in a calm, even tone. "We've traveled the world. We've been to amazing places, and we're just getting started on this new journey of driving around the country. We love each other more and more every day. That's more than a lot of people can say."

She agreed with him but couldn't disregard the sadness that

had filled her mind. She never could ignore the hole in her heart that used to be filled with the joy of motherhood. "Wouldn't saying no have been easier?"

"No," he answered quietly. "I think if either of us were committed to making it happen, we would have taken the steps by now."

He was right. After she'd had two miscarriages, Tobias insisted they wouldn't try again. However, they'd never even researched what other options they had. They'd never have children. Carol would never be a mother again. She had to admit, part of her was relieved. Losing Katie had nearly destroyed her. The miscarriages had been devastating. The reason Tobias had insisted they wouldn't try again was because he was scared for her physical and mental health.

There were other ways they could have had a family, but the fear of losing another child always lingered in her mind and prevented her from moving forward. She'd always be terrified, more than most parents. That would have taken a toll on her and their child. She would have been one of those annoying helicopter parents who never let her kid out of her sight.

Maybe things were better this way.

"I wanted to," she said. "You would have been an amazing father."

He tightened his hold on her hand. "I'm not sorry, and I don't regret the choices we've made, so don't go down that road."

"What road?" she asked, knowing exactly what he was saying.

"I wanted to have children with you, but that didn't happen.

That doesn't make me want this life any less, so don't start thinking I shouldn't have chosen you."

Damn it. As much as she relied on his ability to read between her lines, she despised how easily he could. "I hate you sometimes," she whispered.

"No, you don't. You couldn't live without me any more than I could live without you." Tugging her hand, he waited for her to glance at him. "I couldn't live without you. I wouldn't ever want to. This"—he gestured at the world around them—"is what I want. This is enough for me. Let this be enough for you too."

"This is enough," she said. "I guess we'll have to keep spoiling Elijah and Lara's girls." She couldn't help but smile when she thought of her nieces. Tobias's younger brother and his wife had three daughters now, and Carol adored each one. The girls, even though they were young, knew they had their aunt wrapped around their fingers. She didn't mind. In fact, she cherished the bond they shared.

Tobias nodded. "That's a good plan. I think we should make a list of all the places we'd like to see. Maybe we can add a stop or two for the girls. We can take them on a trip over the summer. They'd love that."

A memory, a flash of the past, hit Carol like a burning arrow. Katie had a list. Carol and her ex-husband had promised to take their little girl on their first real vacation. Though she and John couldn't afford a trip, she'd never taken a childhood vacation, and she wasn't going to deprive her daughter of that joy. Even though the budget was small, Katie had been so excited when she'd been told to pick a few places she'd like to visit.

*She'd made a list in red crayon. The list was too long, but Carol hadn't told her that. She hadn't wanted to dampen Katie's happiness. They'd never taken that vacation. Katie had died before they could. But Carol could remember, clear as day, how Katie had sat at the kitchen table with all her books about America scattered about as she picked what she thought would be the very best places to see.*

*Pushing the shock of the memory down, Carol blew out a shaky breath, but her heartache remained, and tears fell down her cheeks.*

*"Hey," Tobias said gently.*

*She laughed lightly before wiping her tears away. "Katie had a list for the vacation we were planning. She wanted to go so many places. She was so full of curiosity."*

*"So, pick a place for Katie," he said. "We'll go there next."*

*After clearing her throat, Carol said, "Mount Rushmore. She was the most excited about Mount Rushmore. She couldn't believe faces could be carved in a mountain." Carol smiled. "But she called it Mount Hushmore, even when I corrected her."*

*Tobias kissed the back of Carol's hand. "Mount Hushmore it is."*

*"And then maybe the Grand Canyon?"*

*He beamed. "Man, Katie knew how to plan a trip."*

*"Yeah, she did." Carol gazed out at the rising sun. "She would have loved this. She would have..." Her words faded, and she swallowed hard. "I almost said she would have been in heaven here."*

*Tobias set his coffee on the ground and scooted his chair against hers so he could drape his arm over her shoulder. He pulled her closer and kissed her head. He didn't say anything. He'd learned long ago there was nothing he could do to console her when the memory of Katie surfaced. The best thing he could do was let her feel the pain, cry the tears, and then help her refocus when she was ready.*

———

Carol sat at the table of her RV, turning Mei's worry stone over and over in her hand.

*No Regrets.*

She was overanalyzing the meaning of those two words. She overanalyzed everything.

As they'd eaten dinner, Harold had told her he was leaving in the morning. They'd have breakfast as they had the previous two days, and then he'd unhook his RV and hit the road. He was headed toward Nevada, where he'd spend the holidays with his family. Then, after the New Year, he'd head back out to destinations unknown.

She was sad to see him go. She'd grown fond of him over the last few days. They seemed like kindred spirits in many ways. He understood the paradox she'd found herself in— knowing she had to pick up and move on but not having a clue how to. Or the willpower to try.

Imagining the sunbeams they'd seen earlier in the day, she dared to think Tobias had sent Harold her way, that he'd had some divine hand in sending a stranger to save her from herself and give her a nudge in the right direction. That would be just like Tobias. Subtle but effective.

Though Carol had turned off the notifications on her phone after speaking to her mom earlier, her smartwatch vibrated, letting her know she was getting a call. The little screen filled with the name of the person disrupting her deep thought.

Simon Miller.

Seeing his name brought mixed emotions. Long ago, she and Simon could spend hours talking about anything. They'd recently renewed their friendship when Simon accepted Carol's donation to the children's hospital in Dayton. After John had died, she'd had their old house remodeled. She'd dubbed it Katie's House and donated it to the hospital for families to stay while their child received treatment.

Though she'd only seen Simon briefly at the dedication ceremony for Katie's House, talking with him now was like twenty-four years hadn't passed them by. But, much like Tobias, Simon was too good at calling her out on her shit, and she wasn't sure she was up for that right now. Sometimes, wallowing was easier—not healthier or more productive, but definitely easier.

Carol debated letting his call go to voice mail, but if she didn't answer, he'd worry. She didn't want that. Clearing her throat, she forced herself to sound chipper as she answered. "Hey."

"Hey." His deep voice sounded a bit gravelly.

Though he'd only said that one word, Carol had heard the stress. Years ago, when they'd worked together at a children's hospital, she'd hear that same strain in his voice when one of his patients was losing a battle. Though he was the chief of staff now, no longer working with patients, his job was just as stressful in different ways. Clearly he'd had a bad day.

Instantly, she was able to shift her self-pity into concern for Simon. "You sound tired," she said.

"Long day. How was yours?" As expected, he deflected. He never wanted to talk about his bad days.

"Not too bad," she said. "I took a nice long hike this morning and played cards with a few other travelers this afternoon. They have a nice little community area here."

"I'm glad you're socializing," he said. "I worry about that."

Carol chuckled. "You sound like my mother."

Simon laughed as well but only for a moment. "I'm sorry I didn't call you yesterday. I got stuck in meetings. By the time I got home, I was worn out."

Carol started to remind him he didn't have to call her at all, let alone on a schedule. Nor did he owe her an explanation for not calling. Before the words left her, he continued.

"How was your rafting trip?" he asked.

"I didn't go," she confessed.

She was met with silence and was reminded of how thoughtful Harold had been before pointing out what a horrible idea that had been for her to even try. Unlike Harold, Simon knew the reasons why being near water was so traumatic for Carol. When she'd told him that she'd chosen this campground so she could take a trip on the water, he'd tried to be supportive. He'd reminded her how to work through anxiety, how to redirect her thoughts if things became overwhelming, and nicely told her changing her mind was okay.

Simon had never tried to talk her out of making mistakes. He did his best to be supportive even when he thought she was wrong and then did his best to help her pick up the pieces. Even after all this time, Carol could see the old, comfortable patterns at play. Other than Tobias, Simon was the only person who knew when and how to support her without making her feel incompetent.

"I got there," she said, knowing he was waiting for more information, "and filled out the waiver, but when the time came time...I chickened out."

"*Chickened out* is a harsh way to put it," he said.

"I don't think so."

"*I* do," Simon countered, his voice firm despite his obvious exhaustion. "Your trauma blocked your ability to move forward. That's different than simply being too scared to try something new. You have a very good reason to fear the water."

She rolled her eyes and smirked. "Don't get all psychological. Please. You know I hate that."

"You hating my approach doesn't mean I'm wrong. In fact, your resistance to my wisdom implies I'm correct."

Laughing, she turned in the small booth seat and leaned against the wall. "I don't need you picking my brain apart. I do that all day long and half the night when I can't sleep."

"Have you tried meditating before bed?"

Rubbing her thumb over the worry stone, she sighed.

"I'm terrible at meditation. I can't stop thinking long enough to not think."

"Meditation isn't about stopping your thoughts—"

"It's about bringing them back," she finished. "Trust me, I've read the books and listened to the lectures. My friend Alyssa has been meditating for most of her life. She's tried to help me learn how to quiet my mind, but I just can't. I'm simply not good at it."

Rather than argue with her, as she figured he would, he said, "I'm glad you didn't go rafting."

"Why's that?"

"Because there is absolutely no reason why you should put yourself through that. You don't have to prove anything to anyone. Everyone knows how strong you are."

She closed her eyes and rested her head against the wall. Everyone was constantly telling her how strong she was, how much strength she had in order to overcome so many tragedies. She didn't feel strong, and *trying* was a bar set too far out of her reach right now. Right now, she was just trying to keep moving.

"Everyone but *you*," Simon added.

There he went, calling her out as he had for as long as she'd known him. She wasn't really in the mood for that.

Carol set the rose quartz aside and slid from the booth. If she was going to get through this conversation, she would want a glass of wine. "I've spent a lot of time over the last year coming to terms with things," she said as she grabbed a bottle from the fridge. "I've recognized that I can't keep pretending everything is okay when it's not. I've finally allowed myself to mourn for Katie. My mother and I have never been closer. I've let go of old resentments that had been weighing me down for years. But you know what I haven't been able to come to terms with yet?" she asked as she poured more rosé in the wineglass than she likely needed.

"Losing your husband," Simon said softly.

Hearing him say the words made her chest ache and her eyes burn. "I'm so lost right now," she admitted. She took a drink as she listened to the quiet on the line. "For some reason, I thought climbing into a raft and going over rapids was going to get me over this emotional blockage that's preventing me from processing his death."

"You and Tobias had a great life together," Simon offered, even though she hadn't ever really delved into her marriage with him. He knew she loved her husband, but he didn't know the millions of reasons why. "His loss was tragic and unexpected. You can't put a time limit on grieving for that."

"This isn't about putting a limit on my grief, Simon. It's about my inability to feel things that hurt." Sitting back in the booth, she stared at Mei's stone but didn't pick it up. Holding the gift felt like a betrayal to Harold's strength when she could actually feel herself slipping into her negative thought patterns. "I had to protect myself emotionally from my parents as a kid. I had to learn to shut down so their words couldn't hurt me. I've never unlearned that. Even now, turning off my emotions is my go-to when things get difficult. I'm more than halfway through my life. It's time to break that cycle, but hell if I can figure out how." Finding a therapist was a step in the right direction, but she wasn't ready to share that decision just yet. Simon was a doctor. He wouldn't judge her, but Carol wasn't comfortable sharing how far she'd fallen.

"Go easy on yourself, Caroline," he said.

Simon was the only person who called her by that name. She'd stopped using her given moniker when she'd left her old life behind. When she'd walked away from her ex-husband and the memory of finding her daughter's lifeless body, she'd walked away from being *Caroline*. However, Carol had come to realize her former self wasn't as far in the past as she'd pretended for so many years. Caroline's memories had a way of sneaking up on Carol and kicking her feet from beneath her. Those memories were like monsters hiding in the shadows, ready to pounce and shred her to pieces when she least expected it. She'd made peace with John, their mistakes, and Katie's passing. Even so, some memories would haunt her forever.

One of the barriers she'd put between herself and the past in a weak attempt at protecting herself was insisting no one called her Caroline. However, when she'd unexpectedly reconnected with Simon, hearing him call her Carol was wrong. That name didn't sound right coming from him. Simon was the one bright spot in Carol's past that hadn't been marred by John's drinking or Katie's death. When Simon called her out of the blue one day, she realized she could think of him and feel that same sense of peace wash over her.

"Why do you sound so tired?" she asked, redirecting the conversation.

He let out a miserable groan, and she pictured him dragging his hand over his face. Though they were both older now, she pictured him as the younger version of himself, the one she'd known, rather than gray-haired and sporting a short beard.

"I spent most of my day in budgeting meetings," he said. "You know that old saying, trying to squeeze blood out of a turnip? Well, I'm the turnip now."

She smiled at his assessment, but there was more. Their time together years ago gave her insight to his Simon's inner workings, and he wasn't being completely honest with her. "What else?"

"That's not enough?"

"Yeah," she said gently, "that's enough, but there's something else. What's bothering you?"

After a few drawn-out seconds, he said, "I don't know why I took this position." His confession was soft, in that unguarded voice he used to use when they were hiding from the world and could be genuine with each other. "I thought I was going to make a difference, I guess. I'm not. I'm running in the same circles as my predecessor, making the same mistakes, hearing the same bullshit he had to hear."

"First, I'm going to point out that you *do* make a difference," she stated firmly.

"Not like I did when I was working with the kids."

Carol understood that feeling more than he probably realized. She'd changed directions after losing her daughter.

Rather than becoming a pediatrician like she'd planned since she was in middle school, she'd spent decades working her way up to an executive position at a pharmaceutical company. "You know, the first time I went to work after Katie died, I knew I couldn't do the job I'd dreamed of doing. I couldn't let myself lose someone again. I couldn't watch another child die. Changing directions wasn't what I'd planned, but the position I ended up in was crucial. I still helped people, Simon. My job was different, my focus was on something else, but I helped so many people by ensuring the medications they needed were safe. I still saved lives. You might not be hands-on with the kids anymore, but you're protecting the hospital and the doctors the patients need. You're providing them a safe place to heal. Your job matters. You're *still* helping them."

He was quiet for a few seconds before saying, "Thank you. I needed to hear that."

"I figured you did."

"All those years I spent griping about how the executives didn't get what we were going through... I thought I'd step in and make changes. I didn't realize choosing which department would receive what they needed and which would go without would be so difficult."

Carol smirked, knowing he'd hate her solution, but she had to say it anyway. "You can make cuts, skip bonuses, and forgo raises for a time. That's what executives usually do."

He moaned miserably. "That'll go over well. They'll really love me then."

"Are you there to help the hospital or to be admired?"

"Ouch."

"That psychoanalysis thing goes both ways," Carol teased.

Simon chuckled. "I'm there for the kids. And the staff."

Carol's smile softened as she reminded him of a hard truth. "Sometimes, that means making tough calls that won't be popular with the very people you're trying to protect."

"I know," he said. "I hate it, but I know. Let's talk about something less depressing. Tell me about your day and all your adventures."

"My adventures aren't as exciting as you're probably imagining."

"I don't know. I mean, I read four grant summaries today and ate cold alphabet soup for lunch. Your adventures have to be more exotic than that. What did you eat for lunch?"

She sipped her wine before answering, "Carrot sticks and leftover chicken salad."

"Never mind," Simon deadpanned. "You *are* boring."

Carol laughed heartily. "Well, I had raisins in my oatmeal for breakfast. That was a break from the norm."

"Pace yourself, Caroline."

"I can't. I'm a woman on the edge."

"I sense that about you." His voice had changed. The strain had left, replaced by the lighter sound that Carol had been so drawn to from the day she'd met him. On one hand, she was happy to hear the change, but deep down, part of her hated that she was so in tune with him.

Simon had been a light in the darkness of her life years ago and was starting to become that again. She wasn't sure she was ready to start feeling like he was a beacon in her storm.

Though he didn't call every day like her mother, he called often enough that Carol knew he was checking in on her. He didn't come right out and voice his concerns like Judith was sure to do, but he didn't like Carol being on the road alone either. Rather than nag her about safety and going "home," he asked about her day and her plans for the coming days. That was his subtle way of knowing where she would be should something happen. Though keeping an eye on her wasn't his responsibility, she liked that he took the time. She liked knowing he worried about her more than he should.

Picking up Mei's worry stone now that her mood had lifted, Carol thumbed the letters as she settled in to tell Simon about Harold and their hike and the amazing view from the overlook. She'd tell him in great detail about the trail, the weather, and the views that had taken her breath away.

She'd leave out the part about crying over sunbeams, though. Simon didn't need to know about that.

# THREE

THE DAY after Harold left the campground, Carol moved on too. The next stop on her list was Arches National Park in Utah. There, she stood silently, staring up at the natural wonder that was Turret Arch. Though this was the smaller of the arches along the trail, the holes created in the sandstone by centuries of erosion were amazing.

As awe-inspiring as the structure was, her mind was elsewhere. She'd had her first counseling session early that morning. As soon as Dr. Baxter had appeared in their video chat, Carol had immediately fallen into her robot persona. With a faked smile and perfectly timed nods, she'd shared only what was asked. That was how she got through uncomfortable situations.

Dr. Baxter caught on to her game quickly and pointed out what Carol was doing. Though Carol understood she needed to be called out in order to break the habit, she fumbled when she was put on the spot like that. Years of trauma from her father's gruff approach to raising her would surface, and she'd freeze. She could see how things would play out in a flash before her eyes and behave in a way that she anticipated would cause the least amount of conflict. It was the same response she'd had when she was faced with the reality of white-water rafting.

Dr. Baxter had pushed gently. Coaxed kindly. And Carol had broken down.

She'd been so embarrassed, but Dr. Baxter had reassured her that was what she needed. She needed to break down. She needed to lay her pain bare. She needed to expose her wounds so they could heal. Breaking down was perfectly normal during the healing process, according to Dr. Baxter. Carol didn't feel normal. She'd never felt normal. Apparently *that* was normal too. Carol had assumed her ability to turn herself to stone was some kind of superpower, but she wasn't that special after all. Dr. Baxter said that was a common defense.

The funny thing was, Dr. Baxter hadn't said anything Carol didn't already know. She'd told herself these things a thousand times, but having someone who didn't know her validate them made accepting them easier.

The floodgates on her pain had opened months ago when John resurfaced in her life. He'd found her living in Houston, hiding from the past, and made her confront the loss of their daughter. He'd been terminally ill and was running out of time. Carol had to choose between continuing to overlook how much darkness she was keeping inside or helping John confront their past. She'd chosen the latter. By the time he'd died, they'd made peace with each other, but Carol was, once again, left holding an overflowing bag of trauma. She'd done her best to sort through the feelings on her own. Now, she'd connected with someone who could help her get through the rest. Dr. Baxter had pushed when she sensed Carol was holding back. That in and of itself made Dr. Baxter seem the right person for the job.

Not many could see through Carol's cool exterior. Then again, that cool exterior was showing cracks from the strain. Too much of the past was coming to the surface. Without Tobias there to help her pull herself together, she was fraying. Her family had seen the signs months ago. Now, Carol had to admit she was seeing them too.

A lifetime of avoiding the water hadn't helped her heal. She'd only managed to ignore what everyone else could see.

She was broken. She had been for as long as she could recall.

"Beautiful, isn't it?" a gravelly voice asked, distracting Carol from the looping instant replay of her therapy session.

Carol nodded at a woman beaming from beneath a wide-brimmed army green hat. Long black hair fought against the braids the frizzy strands had been wrangled into. The woman was several inches shorter than Carol, but her personality was bursting, from wide eyes to wild gestures.

"Yes," Carol said. "It's amazing."

"Are you here alone?" the woman quizzed, as if the question weren't at all out of place. "I only ask because I am," she continued when Carol hesitated, "and I wanted to hike to Delicate Arch. That's a tough trail, and even though it's

A LIFE WITHOUT REGRETS

usually busy, I'm in search of a hiking partner in case I do something stupid like fall off a cliff or break an ankle." The woman smiled wide, exposing stained, yellow teeth. "I'm not selling this well, am I? Let me try again."

Carol glanced down when the hiker stuck her tanned hand out. From the appearance of her leathery skin, she'd spent quite a bit of her time basking in the sun. She was probably an expert at tackling trails, which made her request even more odd.

"Gillian Bianchi," the woman stated. "Lone adventurer in search of another lone adventurer—preferably a fellow female—for the next three hours or so. Safety in numbers, sister."

Carol couldn't help but smile. The first time she'd met her friend Alyssa was at a park in Houston. Carol and Tobias had just moved to the city, and Carol had researched the safest parks to jog by herself. Tobias couldn't always be with her. The first time she went to a trail close to their home, she was stretching when a petite brunette walked right up to her.

Alyssa Gilmore had done much as Gillian had; she shoved her hand out and introduced herself. She'd told Carol she didn't mind running alone but preferred having a partner because it was safer for women to travel in packs. Hearing Gillian say much the same thing warmed Carol's heart as she thought of her friend.

Holding her hand out, Carol returned the handshake. "Carol Denman."

"You got anything better to do today than make sure I don't die in the wilds of Utah, Carol?"

59

A smirk tugged at Carol's lips. "I guess that depends. When you say it's a tough trail, how tough are you talking?"

Gillian dug in the pocket of her gray cargo pants and pulled out a map from the visitor center. Unfolding the pages, she excitedly pointed out the steep climbs and rock ledges that tripped up many beginner hikers. Though Carol's heart ticked a bit with apprehension, there wasn't a single rapid or inflatable raft between them and Delicate Arch. There was no reason Carol should turn away from this hike, other than the overpowering personality surging from Gillian, which wasn't a good enough excuse.

Carol, too, was a lone adventurer, but there wasn't much to this journey she was taking if she stuck to the safe trails, which was what she'd been doing all along. All her life, really. Harold had reminded her there were other ways to honor Tobias. She'd known that, but the reminder had been necessary to snap her out of her self-pity after her inability to go rafting.

She'd flaked out on the rafting trip. She wasn't going give herself the opportunity to turn her back on this one. Tobias would have been in absolute awe of the structures that nature had created, and Delicate Arch was the most well-known of all the features in the park. As an environmental scientist, this would have been a haven for him. He would have stood beside her, pointing as he explained how the arches had been created and how they were ever-changing because of the wind. How the sandstone was gradually swept away, and how, someday, these natural wonders would be worn down until nothing remained.

Tobias would jump at this opportunity to hike into the *wilds of Utah*, as Gillian had described them. So, Carol jumped too.

"Let's do it," Carol said.

Gillian pumped her fist into the air. "Yes!"

Carol and Gillian made arrangements to meet at the parking lot closest to the trailhead. Within half an hour, Carol had parked, texted her mother where she was and who she was with, and hopped out of her RV to go hiking on her latest adventure.

"You got water? Sunscreen? A phone?" Gillian asked as she hooked a compass onto her belt loop. As carefree and reckless as Carol thought Gillian seemed when asking a stranger to accompany her on a potentially dangerous hike, Gillian at least had the sense to be prepared.

"All of the above," Carol said. As a precaution, she added, "I've let some friends know where we're headed. If they don't hear from me in a few hours, they'll send out a search party."

Gillian clapped. "Woot! Let's get going."

The path started out smooth, easily conquered by the women as they made small talk. Gillian had never been married—never had a need to, according to her. She'd been a computer programmer for years before selling everything and hitting the road, much like Carol had. Unlike Carol, Gillian seemed to have found herself while roaming alone. As she boasted about how free she was with no one to answer to, Carol ruminated about how much she missed having someone to spend her time with. She missed having a partner in her travels. Maybe that was why she was so open to Simon checking on her, despite there not being a need for him to. Having someone show he cared, even with a simple phone call, was nice.

If Tobias were here, they'd be hiking this same trail, but Carol had no doubt she'd be enjoying his company much more. That wasn't a slight to Gillian, simply a fact. Tobias's enthusiasm was an elixir for Carol. Hearing him ramble off facts as he pulled her to a stop to examine a plant or rock had made her ridiculously happy. Whenever he got out into nature, he was like a kid. So excited, so eager to share what he knew.

She'd loved that about him.

"This is the life," Gillian said, slightly winded as they started up an incline in the path. "Nobody telling me where to be, when to be there. I spent too long living by someone else's clock. Know what I mean?"

"I never minded having a schedule," Carol said. "I liked the structure."

"Not me. No, ma'am. I'm a loner. Always have been. The man has kept me down long enough."

Carol smiled in response, mostly because Gillian said the words with too much enthusiasm, like she'd practiced the speech a hundred times before giving it. Though Gillian marched forward, head high, looking every bit like she believed the words coming from her mouth, Carol sensed she didn't. Gillian most likely had practiced this mantra so much because she didn't believe it. Saying the words over and over would make them true. Eventually.

Carol knew because she'd played that game a thousand

times too. One of the many bad habits she had to break, according to Dr. Baxter, was lying to herself until the falsehood became reality. As the doctor pointed out, the truth surfaced sometime. Right now, Carol was finally facing the reality that Tobias was gone. Really gone.

No more pretending he was on a business trip or visiting family. Over a year had gone by. She had to face the fact that he was never going to come back to her, not even if she went rafting.

"Check that out," Gillian said, once again distracting Carol from her thoughts. Gillian pointed at the valley of sand and shrubs. "Nothing but rattlesnakes and scorpions could call a place like this home. Where are you from?"

"Houston," Carol said as they continued the path.

"Oh, the humidity of Southern Texas. My hair is kinky enough without the humidity."

"I don't have that problem," Carol said, pointing at her straight, shoulder-length hair. "I don't miss the humidity. But I do miss the city more than I expected I would. I was never keen on the noise and the constant rush when I lived there, but all that becomes a part of you after a while."

"Never could stand the sounds of urban living. I'm from Northern California."

Carol's spirits lifted, picturing the green rolling hills of Napa Valley. She and Tobias had spent a week there once, wine tasting and having romantic dinners on the veranda of their cottage. She blinked the memory away before saying, "The land of wineries."

"I prefer a strong Irish whiskey," Gillian countered. "I like to know I'm drinking something."

Carol stifled a chuckle. She could almost picture the woman next to her taking a swig and letting out one of those telltale sighs as the alcohol burned its way to her stomach. She knew then that this chance meeting wasn't like the first time she'd met Alyssa. She and Gillian wouldn't form some unbreakable bond. They were two ships passing in the night.

Distracted by a loud round of laughter, Carol watched a group of young men tempting fate by stepping to the very edge of a steep rock face and peering down. Though the trail was several feet wide, one wrong move and someone could tumble over the edge, which was the reason Gillian had asked for company, someone who could call for help if she fell.

"Risky business right there," Gillian said.

"To be so young and stupid," Carol replied as they trekked on.

"The bad thing is, that kind of recklessness is encouraged by our society. Social media has made being stupid a badge of honor."

Carol took a drink of her water as she listened to Gillian's long list of ways technology was ruining the world. Carol couldn't disagree with most of them. She'd avoided social media as much as possible. She'd rather send a text or e-mail to stay in touch, but she understood the draw for most people. Perhaps if she didn't have a tendency to dissociate, as Dr. Baxter had called it, Carol would be more inclined to enjoy sharing her life with the world. Not that she had much of a life to share these days.

"I'm telling you," Gillian continued, "we had it made back in our day when we didn't have to try to compete with everyone else's lives."

"Oh, I think we tried to," Carol said, "only not on such a grand scale."

"Not me. I never tried to fit in. I liked being the outcast. Still do."

Gillian put on what Carol was starting to recognize as her facade. While Carol hid behind a polite but frozen face, Gillian put on a bright, beaming grin and forced excitement. She embraced being on the outside rather than fighting to get where she wanted to be. Carol did her best to fit in, to be the person others wanted her to be, so she didn't disappoint them. It seemed to her that Gillian fought to *not* be who she wanted to be so she didn't disappoint herself.

Gillian was obviously lying to herself about how much she enjoyed the freedom of being on the road as much as Carol lied to herself about being okay. There was something as lonely and broken inside Gillian as there was inside Carol. They were different sides of the same coin.

"Do you have family?" Carol asked.

"A brother I don't see much of. You?"

"My mom and aunt. Some cousins and in-laws."

"Oh, you're married." The way Gillian said the words sounded more like disillusionment than a mere observation. Apparently, Carol's appeal lessened with the prospect of being in a relationship.

Though she was tempted to enthusiastically start rambling about her amazing husband, she said, "Widowed."

Then the inevitable question came. "Do you have kids?"

"No," Carol said instead of rehashing her painful past.

"Me either. Never wanted any. Who needs that kind of financial and emotional burden?"

Rather than counter Gillian's bleak outlook on human connections and familial ties, Carol half listened as she walked beside her hiking partner. Gillian seemed perfectly content to ramble on, which Carol decided was further proof of the woman's loneliness. Why else would she feel the need to talk so much? She clearly was desperate for someone to hear her. Carol was okay with being that someone for a while, at least on the surface.

In her mind, however, Carol was once again imagining how excited her husband would have been if he were the one walking beside her. He'd be telling her about the layers in the rock and how the wind and rain had formed this valley. He'd quiz her, and his face would light up when he came to something she didn't know. He was a know-it-all, but not in a cocky way. In a way that made her want to hear what he had to share. About everything. His need to share what he knew was charming. Infectious.

Like his smile.

"Well, I'll be," Gillian said with awe rather than the forced excitement she'd been using to insist how much she loved her freedom.

Carol gasped as she gazed at the free-standing arch they were approaching. The naturally carved sandstone rose proud and defiant against the bright azure sky. Layered plateaus and snowcapped mountains stood in the distance, as if they too couldn't quite believe what they were seeing.

The scene was spectacular. Knowing nature had provided the arches without the help of man was humbling.

"Oh my God," Carol whispered as she put her hand to her heart. "You'd love this," she said to Tobias.

Unlike when she'd stood in awe of the view with Harold, Carol suppressed the urge to shed some tears for Tobias. Gillian didn't seem the type to offer a comforting hug to a mourning widow.

Reaching into her pocket, Carol squeezed the rose quartz worry stone and rubbed her thumb over the engraving. Much like when she spotted the sunbeams, Carol felt Tobias was there with her, seeing what she was seeing, feeling as impressed by the view.

Harold was right. He was *so* right. There were a thousand ways Carol could honor Tobias. This was definitely one of them.

———

*Carol glanced at her clock to check the time when her cell phone rang. Again. She didn't need to check the caller ID to know the call was from Alyssa. Again.*

*Carol's best friend was nothing if not persistent. Ever since Tobias had died, Alyssa couldn't simply leave a voice mail like a normal person. She called over and over and over until Carol answered the phone.*

However, Carol ignored this call as she had the last three, only this time she put the ringer on mute. If she didn't stay focused, she was going to miss something in the report she was reviewing and lose several hours' worth of work.

Carol read each word on the page carefully. Slowly. Analyzing every letter. Absorbing every detail. She was so focused, she literally squealed when someone knocked on her bedroom door.

Jolting, she jerked her head and up and focused on Alyssa standing there, holding a bag and a drink tray from a local deli. Carol exhaled loudly when her heart started beating again. "What the hell are you doing?"

"Since you haven't been answering my calls, I thought you must be dead," Alyssa said flatly. "I came to clean out your jewelry box before calling the cops."

One of the reasons she and Carol became such close friends was because they shared the same brand of humor, which was slightly off-color and usually a bit on the dry side.

"I'm busy," Carol countered. "Clean out the box and go. The good stuff is in the safe downstairs, though."

Alyssa tossed the bag onto the bed and started pulling off her jacket. Though Alyssa was at least six inches shorter than Carol, her cocked brow and deep scowl were intimidating. "Why aren't you answering my calls?"

Carol gestured to the papers scattered around her. "I'm working. A new drug study was released. I have to read it, understand it, and be able to ask the appropriate questions by the end of the week."

"For three days?" Alyssa said with blatant accusation in her tone. *"You've been working so much for three days that you can't stop long enough to let me know you're okay?"*

*Carol sat a bit taller. "I didn't realize I have to check in with you."*

*"Well, you do. For the record, you do have to check in with me." Opening the bag, Alyssa peered in. "When was the last time you ate?"*

*Carol had to think about that. Dinner? No. Lunch? No, she'd passed on going out with her coworkers. "I had an apple."*

*"When?"*

*"This morning."*

*"Jesus Christ, Carol. What are you doing to yourself?"*

*Carol rolled her shoulders back, bracing for the attack. She and Alyssa had never really fought, but Carol knew that tone. Tobias used to use that tone when he was trying to push her. Her mother used that tone when she was fed up with what she considered to be Carol's "antics." Whenever Carol attempted to think for herself and dared to challenge what her mother insisted was best for her, Judith would get a snappy tone with just enough disappointment to cut down Carol's confidence.*

*"Have you looked at yourself lately?" Alyssa asked. "You're about two shades paler than a sheet of notebook paper, and the bags under your eyes are big enough to pack for a trip to Europe."*

*Carol's mouth fell open as she widened her eyes. "If you came here to criticize me—"*

*"I came here—"*

*"—you can leave," Carol stated loudly to drown out whatever excuse her friend was about to come up with.*

Alyssa didn't leave. In fact, she pulled a cup from the drink carrier and took a long drink as she stared Carol down. "I'm allowed to worry about you," Alyssa stated after swallowing her big gulp. "That's what friends do."

"Worry about what? I'm fine."

Shaking her head, Alyssa reached into the bag and held out a sandwich. Carol stared at the food for a few seconds before her stomach won out and she grabbed it. She didn't even care what she was eating. She just needed to eat something.

"If you need to hide behind your work to process losing Tobias, then you do that," Alyssa said, digging for her own sandwich, "but don't you dare make me worry about you like this again. That's not fair to me."

"I'm sorry," Carol said, unwrapping what turned out to be turkey on sourdough. "I tend to get focused, and everything else falls away."

"You can't do that to me, okay? I was really getting scared."

"Okay," Carol said softly.

"I'm not going to try to tell you how to get through this," Alyssa said, "but I need to know you are getting through."

Leaning over, Carol hugged her friend, grateful that at least one person wasn't going to try to give her all the answers. "I'm getting through," she said, although she didn't really believe that. The world had cracked beneath her feet and she was falling. She started to say so to Alyssa, but the words wouldn't form. The confession felt too heavy to share.

Rather than reach out for the help she was becoming more and more aware she needed, Carol pushed her fear down and

*focused on soothing Alyssa's. Carol was much better at
pretending to be okay than admitting she wasn't.*

———

Once again, Simon sounded exhausted when Carol
answered his call. The budget meetings were taking a toll on
him. Carol sympathized as he debated what his next move
should be and the expected fallout of each possible plan.

Six years into the job, and he seemed to have lost touch
with the reason he'd accepted the position in the first place.
Rather than remind him again of the good he could do, she
listened, offered input when asked, and let him work through
his frustration on his own. There wasn't much she could do
other than listen.

"I'm sorry," he said after a few minutes. "I must be driving
you crazy with this."

Sliding into the seat at her table, she said, "No, you're not.
I don't mind."

"This has to be boring to you."

"Actually, I miss having these talks."

"You miss talking about corporate conflict?" he asked, his
tone reflecting his disbelief.

"Yeah. This is infinitely better than telling you I walked
miles over rough terrain. Again."

"Hey," Simon countered. "I like hearing about your day."

"You're using me," she stated.

He scoffed. "How so?"

"To distract you from your problems. You don't give a

damn about how much I went hiking. You just don't want to think about work. But you can't stop yourself."

"Who's doing the psychoanalyzing tonight?"

"It's no fun being on the receiving end, is it?" she asked with a laugh.

"Tell me about your day," Simon insisted.

Carol picked up the turkey sandwich she'd made herself for dinner. "I'm getting lazy. I used to cook several times a week so I'd have leftovers. The last three nights, I've had lunch meat. This is becoming a staple of my diet. That's not a good thing."

"Okay, when I said to tell me about your day," Simon teased, "I meant the hiking and sightseeing part. I don't give a crap about lunch meat."

Carol chuckled and pushed her plate aside before telling him about Gillian and the hike they'd taken. He listened intently, from the odd introduction all the way to when they parted ways with Gillian offering Carol a salute and well wishes for her continued adventures. Carol wrapped up her story with a confession that she could barely walk after the hike to Delicate Arch, despite guzzling water, stretching, and taking ibuprofen for the aches and pains.

"I can tell you one thing," she said. "I won't be hiking *or* sightseeing tomorrow."

"What will you be doing?"

"I'm taking a down day. I think I'll read and enjoy the confines of my RV. I've reserved this spot until the end of the week. I can take time to heal before doing more exploration.

Maybe I'll get around to finding a grocery store and buying some real food."

"Sounds nice," he said. "How long are you planning to be in Utah?"

"Another week or so."

"Where are you headed next?"

"Salt Lake City. I want to wander around the city a bit, maybe visit a museum or two." Carol sat back with her iced tea. "I'll make my way toward St. Louis after that. I'll be staying with Tobias's mother through Thanksgiving. Even though she'd insist it's impossible to overstay my welcome, I don't want to get there too early. I'm planning a few overnight stops along the way."

Simon grew quiet. So quiet, Carol was about to ask if she'd lost him. Finally, he said, "I'm going to be in St. Louis for Thanksgiving. I'm staying with my brother."

He got quiet again, and Carol knew he was about to toss out one of his big ideas. She hated his big ideas, mostly because his ideas kicked her in the ass when she didn't want to be.

When Carol and Simon met two and a half decades ago, she was trapped in a terrible marriage. John had been a functioning alcoholic and consistently made their lives hell. Miserable and lonely, she'd counted on Simon far too much, so much so that they'd ended up having a brief affair. Though their time together hadn't lasted long, the impact had.

Simon was the reason she'd moved to St. Louis.

His big idea back then was for her to leave John. Simon

offered her everything she'd ever wanted, including a house in a wonderful neighborhood where they would have raised her daughter together. He'd even suggested she quit her job as a pediatric nurse and go back to school to get the medical degree she'd said she would finish someday.

She'd turned him down.

Instead of ending her rocky marriage, she'd ended an affair that had made her happier than she'd ever been. She'd stayed with John until their daughter had died. Losing Katie had tipped the scale. She couldn't stay any longer. The night she told Simon she was running away from the life that had hurt her too much, he put together the plan that had saved her. He'd sent her to St. Louis where he used to live. He still owned a house there. He still had connections at the hospital where he'd worked before transferring to Dayton. He gave her a place to live, a place to work, and a way to start her life over.

He'd saved her back then. She assumed he was about to try to save her again. The difference was, despite the pain of her loss, she was stronger now and didn't need to be saved. She needed help; she needed support. But she didn't need him to save her.

"What's going through that big brain of yours, Simon?" she asked when the silence between them dragged on too long.

"A few things."

She smirked at his vague response. "Such as?"

"How would you feel about me flying out to Utah and

doing some exploring with you? We could drive to St. Louis together, and then I'll fly home from there."

Carol's breath caught. The idea of spending so much time with Simon jolted her. Though she knew better than to assume he was suggesting anything more than two old friends traveling together, her mind flashed back in time to when they were lovers. Her heart did a crazy somersault in her chest, and she opened her mouth but couldn't form any kind of response.

"To hang out with you, Caroline," Simon explained. "Nothing more."

"I-I know. But...um..." She scanned the small space around her. The compact RV was the perfect size for two people. The main bed was in the back, and a second bed was above the driving compartment. Though the quarters were close, there was room for two people.

"No," Simon said, interrupting her internal debate. "The word you're looking for is *no*."

Carol closed her eyes and rested her palm to her forehead. "Simon—"

"You're mourning your husband right now."

She dropped her hand and stared at Tobias's photo. "Yeah. I am."

"If you're worried that I'll try to take advantage of you—"

"*No*. I know you better than that," she said. "I trust you. I have mixed feelings about having company right now."

"Company in general or my company?"

"Both," she answered honestly. "I know you're trying to help, and I appreciate your efforts."

"But?"

Carol eyed the photo on the fridge again. "But I miss my husband. You can't fix that."

"I wasn't trying to."

She sighed. She'd hurt his feelings, either by rejecting his offer or implying he was trying to make something better that he couldn't. She started to apologize, but she couldn't make the words come together. She hadn't meant to offend him, but she wasn't sorry for the boundary she'd set.

Spending time with Simon would be wonderful. She loved being around him.

But she was smart enough to know that, honorable as his intentions might be, there would be underlying tension between them. She couldn't say what that tension would be, but they had a past that hadn't ever been fully resolved. She had enough things to settle without allowing Simon Miller to share her space.

"If you decide you want company," he said, "in Salt Lake City or anywhere else along the way, I'd be happy to join you. I'll even bring a tent so I don't invade your space."

She chuckled. "Good to know."

"Do you think we could have dinner since we'll be in the same town?"

"Maybe."

He was quiet again. "Think about it, okay?"

"I will," she agreed. "It's early yet, but I think I'm going to get some rest. My legs are killing me. Thanks for checking in."

"You'll let me know when you get back on the road?"

"Yes. You *and* my mother," she said lightly, hoping to ease the awkwardness between them.

Simon laughed lightly, but the air of discomfort lingered. "Good night."

Carol once again replayed the day's events, from waking up under a cloud of dread all the way to what she'd said to Simon, and her face fell. *I miss my husband.*

Missing Tobias was an understatement. She was lost. Falling through space with no end in sight. She was going to hit bottom eventually. And hitting was going to hurt like hell. She had taken twenty-four years to work up the courage to face Katie's loss. She didn't have another twenty-four years to spare to face losing Tobias.

After putting her dishes in the sink to wash later, Carol crawled onto the bed, stretched out, and stared at the ceiling. Pulling the worry stone from her pocket, she rubbed her thumb over the words as she thought about Gillian and her insistence that she was happy to be free. To be alone. To have no one.

Carol would give anything to have someone. To have Tobias. Katie.

But that was impossible. She had to stop dwelling on how much she wanted the impossible.

As much as she could imagine Tobias with her, standing before some natural wonder and telling her all about it, she could begin to picture Simon. Though she and Simon had never traveled together, that had been something they'd talked about a few times. They liked to talk about a future beyond sneaking off to his apartment when their shifts had ended. Arches National Park had never been mentioned, but Carol could think of him standing at Delicate Arch with her.

"Isn't this incredible?" he would have asked.

That was a phrase Simon used to say often. A patient would make an unexpected recovery, and Simon would beam a brilliant smile as he uttered those words. They'd be curled up together as she kept one eye on the clock, not wanting to go back to reality. He'd pull her closer, kiss her shoulder, and say how lucky they were to have crossed paths.

"Isn't this incredible?" he'd whisper.

What they'd shared had been incredible. Wrong but incredible.

Now that she was considering his offer, she couldn't stop thinking about how this trip would have played out with him. Instead of walking alone, offering shallow greetings to strangers she met on the trails, she could have had company. Real company. Not Gillian and her false bravado.

Carol would have had someone to enjoy her day with. She would have had someone to share *this* day with. More than anything, that was what she'd missed the most— sharing her life with Tobias.

Rolling onto her side, she stared at the photo she kept on the small shelf beside the bed. Blowing out a long, sad exhale as she ran her fingers over his face, she said something she had thought a thousand times but hadn't dared to voice until that moment. "Fuck you for leaving me here all alone, you jerk."

# FOUR

BY THE END of the following week, Carol was back in St. Louis. Home. Or as close as she had to one these days. The bedroom where Tobias had slept right up until they got their first apartment together was hers now. While that offered some comfort to Carol, there was a sadness in her heart every time she entered the room. There was so much of Tobias lingering in this space. His trophies, his posters, his memories. The purity of the love he'd had for everyone he ever met. He had been one of those people who genuinely wanted the best for everyone and was willing to help make that happen if he could. Other than Katie, Tobias had been the closest thing to an angel that Carol had ever met.

Having him in her life had been a blessing. He'd driven her crazy sometimes, but she'd loved him so fiercely, she couldn't imagine ever feeling like that again. She didn't know if she wanted to. That kind of all-consuming love had nearly done her in when she'd lost him. Hell, it continued to do her in. Most days, if she stopped fighting to carry on, even for a minute, she'd lose herself in the grief.

Dr. Baxter had advised her to focus on the good memories while simultaneously making new ones. While her therapist supported Carol's decision to not have Simon travel with her, she was also reminded that she couldn't keep living in the past. Traveling was supposed to be a healing experience for her, not a constant reminder that Tobias wasn't there to see the things she was seeing.

Apparently Carol was clinging to the hurt instead of embracing the opportunity to heal.

Big surprise.

Kneeling on the floor before one of the boxes of memories, Carol hesitated before lifting off the top. The contents had been carefully wrapped in brown paper, so the mementos safely made the transition from her old house in Houston to this tiny room in St. Louis. The first item she unwrapped was a framed photo from her wedding with Tobias. The picture captured a moment when she was leaning into him, her hand resting on his chest as he pressed his cheek to her temple. Their joy was evident and authentic.

They'd promised to do everything in their power to give the other a life of love and happiness, but they couldn't have imagined how amazing the next twenty years were going to be. Despite the ups and downs, they'd both fulfilled that promise until the moment he was ripped out of her life. She couldn't have imagined how someday she'd be sitting in his old bedroom, alone. Widowed. Missing him more with each beat of her heart.

She cradled the photo to her chest and closed her eyes against the burning tears that wanted to form. One of the things Dr. Baxter had been helping Carol learn was how to feel without being consumed.

*Feel the pain; don't live it. Acknowledge the sorrow; don't dwell in it.*

The longer Carol let her hurt be the focus, the longer her pain would linger. She had to learn to acknowledge the loss, feel the emptiness in her heart, and then focus on the happier times so she could be thankful that she'd had them.

The happier times she'd shared with Tobias had been some of the happiest of her life. She'd never been whole after losing Katie, but she was as close as she could have ever been when she'd had the love and support of her husband. From the day they'd met, they'd known each other on a spiritual level. Their souls were meant to be together. They'd fit like puzzle pieces. Instantly.

Her connection to him had saved her from the darkness she'd been living in for so long.

Losing him was more like losing half of herself. Definitely the better, stronger half. Tobias was centered and focused. Carol was good at faking those traits, but inside, she'd been a storm. She'd had a mind filled with chaos and emotional hurricanes swirling below the surface. He'd calmed that. He'd provided a safe haven from her own mind. A haven she had desperately needed then and certainly could use now.

Without him, she'd let the storms back in. The darkness

was closing in, and hard as she tried, she feared she was losing the battle.

Though she still had several boxes to sort through, Carol took the only photo she'd unpacked and crawled onto the bed. With the picture cradled to her chest, she curled into a ball and stared at the place where Tobias used to rest his head. Tears welled in her eyes as she recalled how he would stare up at the ceiling, smiling as he told her stories of his childhood. She'd so loved hearing his stories. Though his father had left when Tobias and his brother, Elijah, were young, Mary had given her sons a happy and healthy childhood. They'd had so many good times, Tobias never ran out of tales to tell.

Carol had been so envious of his stories. Her childhood had been sterile. She'd never had her own memories to share with him, so she'd immersed herself into his. She'd immersed herself into everything about him. Now that he was gone, Carol was starting to realize how much of her had been molded by Tobias. She'd been a self-imposed blank slate when she'd met him.

She'd left Caroline behind her and had yet to figure out who Carol was until Tobias took her hand and pulled her into the light. He'd made her feel like a person again. He'd shown her how to feel again.

How was she supposed to just let that go? He was gone, but in so many ways, he was right there. He was inside her, imprinted on her heart and soul.

Lifting her head when the bedroom door was opened, Carol gestured lamely for her sister-in-law to enter. One of the many things Carol loved about this family was that *in-law* was a technicality. Mary was her mother, Elijah was her brother, and Lara was the sister Carol wished she'd had while growing up. With them, she belonged. She was a part of something larger than herself, part of their orbit.

"I brought whiskey." Lara slipped into the bedroom and closed the door like she didn't want to get caught with the liquor she'd swiped from Mary's cabinet. "May I join you? It was a long day at the office, and drinking alone seems wrong." She kicked off her high heels and started peeling away her blazer before Carol had a chance to answer.

Carol wiped her cheeks as she sat. "I see a bottle but no glasses."

"Glasses are for sissies." Lara climbed onto the mattress, twisted the cap off, and then took a swig. A full-body shiver ran through her as she held the whiskey out to Carol.

"Classy, as always." Carol toasted Lara and then took a drink. The liquor burned all the way down to her stomach. She winced, sighed, and then swallowed another mouthful. After a long exhale, she examined the bottle in her hand. "I met a woman in Utah who said she preferred whiskey over wine. *Why?*" she asked before taking another drink to test what she already knew—she wasn't a fan of whiskey. "*Ugh.* This is awful."

"Okay." Lara reached for the bottle. "Don't get drunk before dinner. Mary will kill me."

Carol grinned as she imagined for a moment the hell Mary would give them if they got sloshed. However, her lips fell quickly because those lectures were usually saved for the troubles that Tobias and Elijah used to get into. "Her name was Gillian, and she made this big show about how independent she was. Nobody told her what to do." Carol smiled, but the grin didn't last. "She was sad. She did her best to hide it, but she was sad. And lonely. I felt sorry for her," Carol said flatly. "But maybe she was on to something. Part of me wishes I didn't have all this…" She gestured around the room.

"Family?" Lara pressed.

Tears sprang to Carol's eyes. "No. That's not…" She blew out her breath. "Ignore me. This year seems harder than last. The shock has worn off. I can feel his absence now, and I really wish I couldn't."

Lara capped the bottle and set the whiskey on Tobias's nightstand before stretching onto her side. She propped up her head on her hand and gave Carol a sympathetic frown. "Nothing screams 'look at my shitty life' like society insisting this is the most wonderful time of the year."

Staring at the boxes of memories, Carol let the photo she'd been holding fall to the side. Furrowing her brow, she muttered, "You think my life is shitty?"

"No," Lara said quickly. *Too* quickly. "No. That's not what I mean. I… I was trying to empathize. I'm sorry."

"Don't be. My life *is* shitty." Carol's lip trembled as she focused on the stack of boxes. "Shitty and…empty."

"It's not empty," Lara said.

Carol chuckled wryly as she took in the concern on Lara's face. "So you *do* think it's shitty."

Lara glared, but a smirk toyed at the corner of her mouth. "*Stop.* I'm not catering to your pity party."

Falling back onto the bed next to Lara, Carol focused on the ceiling like Tobias used to do when they'd share this bed. "Sorry. I was eyeballs deep in feeling sorry for myself when you came in."

"I figured as much. That's why I brought whiskey. Mary's worried about you."

"Mary never stops worrying about me. Or everyone else." Rolling her head toward Lara, Carol confided, "She said you've been working late every night."

Lara rolled her eyes. "No, I haven't. Not *every* night."

"Is everything okay?" Carol asked gently. "With you and Elijah?"

"Yeah. We're fine."

The idea of her family falling apart so soon after losing Tobias was a fear she hadn't harbored until Mary had shared her own concerns. Now, that was weighing on Carol as heavily as the impending holidays. Though she knew she'd never lose her bond with Lara and Elijah, she also knew those bonds would change if they divorced. The idea of more change was almost as terrifying to her as letting go of the past. "Are you sure?"

Lara gripped Carol's hand. "We're fine. I have been working late, but not because there's anything wrong. Rumor has it one of the executives is retiring after the New Year. I want his job. More than that, I don't want anyone saying I got his job because I'm a Black woman. They need to know I earned any promotion I get."

"You have earned it," Carol assured her. "You're brilliant. They're lucky to have you."

"You're my sister. You have to say that. They don't."

"The reality is, no matter how hard you work or how much you prove yourself," Carol said sadly, "someone is going to choose to believe you only got ahead because you're a minority. There is *always* going to be someone who disregards your value and sees you as a statistic. You can't escape that. None of us can. Don't waste your energy proving yourself to anybody else, Lara. If you work hard for the job, then you deserve it. Let that be enough."

After a moment, Lara grinned. "Listen to you, sounding so evolved."

Carol rolled her eyes. "I started therapy so my mom would shut up about it." She tasted the lie as soon as the words left her mouth. "No. I started therapy because I...I scared myself."

Lara sat up and focused her intense dark brown eyes on Carol. "What do you mean? What happened?"

"You know how I have this ability to shut down and push through?"

"Yeah."

For a moment, Carol flashed back to sitting on a wooden bench, clutching a clipboard, as a panic attack threatened to overtake her. What the hell had she been thinking? Rubbing her forehead, she forced the memory away. "I tried to go white-water rafting."

Lara stared for several drawn-out moments, as if trying to make sense of what Carol had just said. "What happened?"

"I froze. Like I've never frozen before. I was on the verge of a full-blown meltdown when this elderly man I met intervened and, thank goodness, talked me out of going out on the river."

Worry filled Lara's eyes as she shook her head. "Why would you do that to yourself? Water triggers you. You know this."

Carol swallowed hard, unable to find a logical explanation. "I thought the time had come to face old traumas. I wanted to... I wanted to put some of my demons to rest. I have so many, you know," she said lightly, as if making a joke would lessen the impact of her words. They had the opposite effect.

Lara's eyes saddened as she tilted her head. "That's not how to face your traumas, Carol."

"I thought I could force myself to stop feeling so screwed up all the time if I finally faced..." Her eyes started to burn, and she silently cursed herself. "I'm so tired of feeling like this."

Lara squeezed Carol's hand. The concern in her dark eyes had grown into what looked like borderline fear. "I get that. I do. But you don't do that kind of stuff alone. You have a family to help you with that. We're here for you. You need to lean on us right now."

"I am."

"No, Carol, you're not," Lara stated. "You're burying yourself in your grief like that's going to make you process it faster."

"I'm trying to figure out how to live without my husband."

"You're running because you aren't willing to face your life without your husband."

Carol scoffed as she sat. With her back to Lara, Carol put her feet on the floor and set the photo of her wedding day on the nightstand. "Way to be supportive," she grumbled.

"I *am* being supportive."

"You sound like my mother, Lara. I don't need to be judged right now." After pushing herself up, Carol headed to the box she'd opened. "You have no idea what I'm going through or how I'm trying to cope."

"You're *not* coping. That's the point."

"I just told you that I've started therapy."

"You're isolating yourself," Lara stated. "That's not healthy."

Facing her sister-in-law with another wrapped frame in her hands, Carol glared. "I'm not isolating myself."

"Traveling alone is the very definition of isolation. Do you want to end up lonely like...that whiskey-drinking loner?"

"Gillian," Carol clarified. "Her name was Gillian. The difference is she chose to be alone. My husband is dead. I don't have any living children. I'm traveling alone because I *am* alone."

Lara's eyes softened into that sympathetic look Carol hated receiving. "You're not alone. You have a family, and we love you. Come home to us. Let us help you."

Furrowing her brow, Carol asked with a sharp tone, "Help me *what*?"

"Grieve. Recover. Live again." Crawling off the bed, Lara

crossed the room in three long strides and pulled Carol into a hug.

Carol tried to pull back before her facade could thaw, but Lara held tight. Closing her eyes, Carol sighed as she melted into the embrace and a surge of emotions made her tears return. Damn it.

"Mary isn't the only one worried about you," Lara said. "Elijah sees what you are going through, and he feels like he's letting Tobias down."

"Oh, don't you do that," Carol said, her voice thick with emotion. Pulling back, she narrowed her teary eyes at Lara. "Don't you dare try to guilt me into getting your way."

"I'm not."

"You just did. You said my problems are making *Elijah* feel bad."

Lara shook her head hard enough to make her shoulder-length black curls bounce. "No, I'm telling you what's going on because you don't seem to be able to see beyond your own pain. Your family is hurting too. We lost Tobias too, Carol. And now, we're losing you."

"You're not—"

"You are pulling away. You are going to that place that only Tobias could reach, but he isn't here to reach you anymore, Carol. You have to let us help you."

"You *can't* help me," Carol insisted on a whisper.

"We can. But you have to let us. You can't really believe driving around in that RV is making this better."

Carol exhaled loudly, suddenly exhausted. "You know, I have to defend my choices to my mother. I'm not defending them to you. I'm not doing this for you. I'm doing this for me."

"Doing *what*?" Lara asked.

Returning her attention to the box, Carol sifted through the contents but didn't really see them. "What am I going to do in St. Louis that I can't do in my RV? What's going to be different if I stay here?"

"The difference is, you'll be surrounded by people who love you. People who miss you."

"That sounds great in theory, but what am I going to do with *me*?"

Lara brushed a tear from Carol's face. "Spa days with your favorite sister. Shopping days with your beloved nieces. Family dinners every Sunday." Lara all but begged, "Come home. Being here isn't the same now. I get that. I do. This isn't what you had planned for your future. This isn't what any of us had planned. If you want to travel, then travel, but don't live alone on the road with nowhere to call home. Not when we want you here. Not when you're still recovering."

Moving around Lara, Carol dropped onto the bed. Pulling the paper from the photo, she sighed. The image peering back at her was of the last anniversary she'd spent with Tobias. Their smiles were so wide, so full of love. "Being here hurts," she confessed. "He's been gone so long now. I can't feel him anymore, Lara."

"You can't run from losing him forever," Lara said gently.

"I'm not running," Carol muttered. "I'm not coping well, but I'm not running."

Lara sat on the bed next to Carol. "What do you call it?"

Carol blinked a few times and then sniffled. "I'm trying to figure out where I belong now."

"You belong *here*," Lara said.

Shaking her head, Carol faced Lara. "Lately... Lately, all this feels like another part of Tobias that I've lost."

"You haven't lost us," Lara said, wrapping her arm around Carol. "You will *never* lose us."

"I don't mean our family. I mean this place. This city. St. Louis used to be our home. I used to feel so at peace here. Even when I was here with John a few months ago, I felt like I was coming home. This time, though... Everything is just a reminder, Lara. Everywhere I go, everything I see, is just a reminder that he's gone. I don't feel at peace anywhere. I don't know where I belong."

"You belong *here*," Lara stated sternly.

Carol set aside the photo and skimmed the room. She didn't want to continue the debate. Lara would never understand the hollow ache in Carol's chest. "I hear what you're saying. I do. The truth is...if I stayed here, Mary would hover. You would hover. I love you guys for worrying, but I have to find my way on my own. I know you want to help, but you can't."

"We'll give you room if that's what you need."

Carol sighed. Lara could say that a thousand times, but Carol knew better. One of the things she loved about Mary was that her maternal instinct ran so deep. She could sense Carol's despair like the pain was her own. Mary would spend every waking moment trying to fix Carol's shattered soul. Carol didn't want or need that kind of attention focused on the pain she was trying to sort through. She'd never been one to lean too heavily on someone, other than Tobias.

Rather than continue talking in circles with her sister-in-law, Carol opted to redirect Lara's attention. "Simon's going to be in town for Thanksgiving. He wants to have dinner."

When Lara didn't respond, Carol glanced over her shoulder. At first, Carol thought maybe Lara didn't know who she meant, even though she'd met Simon a few months before at the ceremony Carol had held to donate Katie's House to the children's hospital. However, she knew Lara remembered the man and how she'd mercilessly teased Carol about how handsome he was. Lara wasn't trying to remember Simon; she was processing some bit of information she'd picked up from Carol's revelation.

"This is what's bothering you, Carol," she said after a few moments. "It's not being here. It's the idea of seeing Simon again. What did you tell him?"

"I told him maybe. But…"

Lara dipped her head down and eyed Carol in the way only a sister can. "*But?*"

"He wanted to fly out to Utah when I was there. He said we could do some exploring together. His suggestion was perfectly innocent. Even so, I told him no. Then, everywhere I went after that, part of me wished he were there. I wished that I weren't alone." Her chest grew tight as her tears returned. "I shouldn't be thinking that."

"Why not?"

Carol looked at her, and Lara wiped a tear off her cheek.

"You think Tobias is gonna get jealous?" Lara asked.

"Think he's gonna care if you're thinking about the future instead of festering in the past?"

"Don't do that," Carol whispered. "Don't dismiss my feelings like that."

"I'm not dismissing anything. I'm trying to make you see that it's okay if you think about someone who's here, someone who can spend time with you. Tobias would want you to move on and be happy. You know that, don't you?"

Carol nodded because she couldn't find her voice, holding back a sob. Moving forward felt like dishonoring two decades with the greatest love of her life. Tobias hadn't even been gone two years. She shouldn't be thinking about a future with anyone.

Brushing her hand over Carol's hair, Lara said, "Have dinner with him. Dinner doesn't mean anything."

"I don't think that's a good idea. I think..."

"What?"

"I used Simon to pick myself up after losing Katie. I'm not going to do that to him again."

Lara was quiet for a moment. "I seem to recall how happy Simon was that he was able to help you. He wasn't resentful or angry that you'd taken the help he'd given you to build a life without him. He seemed like he genuinely cared about you, like we all do. Why won't you let him help you now?"

Carol closed her eyes. Another discussion she didn't want to delve into. "I'll think about it," she said after a few drawn-out seconds. "That's all I can promise right now."

———

*Caroline eased open the door to the hospital roof. Dr. Miller hadn't been seen for quite some time, and she was getting worried. They'd lost one of the patients he'd been treating. The little boy had been admitted with pneumonia several days prior. His health had deteriorated steadily since, but his death had happened suddenly, surprising everyone. Though Dr. Miller hadn't been the boy's primary physician, he'd taken the loss hard.*

*Caroline had been with Dr. Miller when they'd heard the news. She'd seen the way his shoulders had drooped and how the constant sparkle in his eyes dimmed. As soon as the chaos settled, he'd disappeared and hadn't been seen since. She'd been searching the hospital for the last fifteen minutes before finally deciding to check the roof. As soon as she pushed the door open, the wind whipped around her. Though the weather was clear, the tall buildings surrounding them created a wind tunnel effect. The roof always had a steady current.*

*She almost didn't see him standing just outside the amber glow of the lights, but then she noticed movement close to the edge of the building. Narrowing her eyes, she peered into the shadows until she made out his silhouette against the city lights.*

*Letting the door close behind her, Caroline didn't hesitate in heading toward him. Dr. Miller had come to the children's hospital eight months prior. From the day he'd started, she'd felt a level of ease with him that she rarely felt with anyone. The two kept a professional distance, but there was an underlying friendliness there that made her comfortable seeking him out.*

*Stopping at his side, she looked up at his drawn face, even more distressed from the mix of light and shadows. Even when he was troubled, the man was handsome as hell. She probably would have chastised herself for that observation, but he turned his light brown eyes to her, and her breath lodged in her throat. The pain in his gaze pinned her where she stood.*

*Something unspoken passed between them in that instant. There was a silent acknowledgment that they knew each other on a deeper level than they should. They understood each other in a way no one else could possibly understand. The sensation shook Caroline. She creased her brow as the feeling settled over her. She'd never felt this kind of belonging before. The connection made her uneasy because it felt so right.*

*"This is the hard part," he said, pulling her focus from the strange sensation.*

*She couldn't find words to reply. Part of her was analyzing the unexpected moment that had passed between them. She simply nodded and put her hand on his without thinking. The second she touched him, she realized her mistake. However, before she could pull away, he entwined his fingers with hers and tugged her to him. Wrapping his arms around her shoulders, Dr. Miller hugged her tight. Though she shouldn't have, she held him back. Possibly even more closely.*

*He was clearly seeking solace, but Caroline's heart fluttered in an unexpected way. More than once, she'd found herself watching him from across the room. More than once, she'd caught him watching her. Every time, she'd told herself those looks didn't mean anything. Nevertheless, the way her breath suddenly became shallow and the wave of heat that rolled through her told her something completely different.*

*Nothing about the embrace was inappropriate, but her heart started pounding and her knees grew a little weak. Oh. She was in trouble. Her brain told her to step away, to go back inside, to leave him to mourn the loss of his patient on his own. She didn't listen. Instead, she leaned even closer to him, wrapped her arms even more tightly around his waist, and pressed her face into his shoulder.*

*Caroline didn't know how long they'd stood like that, but they'd embraced long enough for her to consider how perfectly their bodies fit together. When he finally pulled back, her arms ached from hugging him so firmly. She would have laughed at herself if he hadn't leaned away just enough to look down at her. The yellowish-brown light caused his eyes to look even more intense.*

*She thought he might kiss her, and she had a flash of all the ways she might react. Certainly, she should tell him no. She was married. Sure, her marriage was a disaster on the best days, but she was married. Another part of her wanted Dr. Miller to kiss her. To make her feel something. Even shame would be better than the emptiness John had left her with for so long.*

*She slid her hand to Dr. Miller's face, and he lowered his gaze to her lips. If she had the courage, she would have made the next move. She would have closed the whisper of a gap between them. But she didn't. As always, she was too scared to take what she wanted.*

*He seemed to be having the same debate, but for him, logic won out. He put a foot or so between them as he lowered his hands. Once again, the wind whipped around Caroline, colder now than even a few minutes ago.*

*"Thank you for checking on me," Dr. Miller said. "I'll be fine. You should get back to work."*

*If not for the obvious longing in his eyes and the yearning in his hug, she might have been offended by his dismissal. He was sparing them both. He was drawing a line she clearly hadn't been willing to draw. Even so, she stood as if she didn't know what she was supposed to do next.*

*Dr. Miller cupped her cheek and lightly brushed his thumb over her skin. "Go inside, Caroline," he said quietly. "I'll be in soon."*

*Swallowing hard, she turned and headed toward the door. As she opened it, she looked back. Dr. Miller had stepped from the shadows to watch her leave. Of course he had. He always watched her leave.*

——————

Carol had avoided answering Simon's calls for two days, blaming her supposed full schedule on her family, but seeing his name on the caller ID first thing in the morning, she knew she couldn't continue to hide from him. The peace she'd found by sitting on Mary's porch watching the sunrise instantly rolled into a ball of nerves in her stomach.

"Good morning," she said after mustering up the courage to connect the call.

"Hey," he said. "I thought you were going to let me go to voice mail. Again."

Despite her determination to be annoyed at his

persistence, she smiled. "I thought about it. I've only had one cup of coffee. I need at least two to fully operate."

"I was hoping to catch you before you got busy."

"Well, you did," she said as she refilled her coffee mug. "How are you?"

"Good," he said. "On my way to work."

"Get the budget stuff worked out yet?"

He laughed wryly. "Are budgets ever worked out?"

"Rarely," she conceded. "However, I have an immense amount of faith in you."

"Well, you're a club of one."

They shared a laugh, but Carol knew the small talk was leading up to the real reason he was calling.

"You never confirmed if I'm going to see you in St. Louis later this week," he said, taking the inevitable turn toward the heart of the conversation.

Carol closed her eyes. "Um, when are you thinking?" She was stalling to scrounge up an excuse to avoid seeing him.

"I fly in Wednesday afternoon, out Sunday morning."

"Oh," she said, faking disappointment. "That's not long, is it?"

"I could stay longer if that means I get dinner out of you."

She smiled despite herself. The last thing she wanted was to let Simon flatter her, but he had a way of doing just that.

"You can say no," Simon offered. "If you're busy or don't want to see me for whatever reason, tell me no, Caroline. That's okay."

Sinking into a chair at the table, Carol let her shoulders sag. "This is only my second Thanksgiving without Tobias. I was so numb last year that I didn't really allow myself to feel it. I don't know how good my company will be, Simon. I'm struggling right now, and I don't want drag you into that."

"I understand," he said gently. "Maybe seeing a friend would help."

"Maybe. Can I call you back this evening and let you know?"

"Of course." He tried to sound upbeat, but she heard the underlying disappointment. "I'm almost to work. I'll chat with you later."

"Okay," she said. "Hey."

"Yeah?"

She opened her mouth but stopped short of telling him she *did* want to see him but she was simply overwhelmed at the moment. Mary shuffled into the kitchen before the words tumbled from Carol's mouth.

Instead of having Mary overhear her confession, Carol said, "Talk to you soon. Bye." She hung up and focused on her mother-in-law. "Good morning."

"Morning, baby," Mary said brightly.

Carol would never understand how the woman woke up so chipper. No matter how early Carol spoke to her, Mary was happy and bright. Carol needed at least one cup of coffee before she could even attempt to be perky, not that she ever really was. She spent too much time lost in her thoughts to find the energy to be so upbeat.

"Was that your mom?" Mary sat across from Carol with a mug in her hands.

"No." For some reason, Carol felt uneasy telling Mary the

truth. There really was no way out of it, though. She could lie or avoid, but Mary would see through her and get the truth anyway. "Do you remember Simon Miller? You met him in Ohio when we were there in September. He was there when we dedicated Katie's House."

"Yes, of course." She turned and gave Carol a wink. "How could I forget that handsome devil?"

Rather than react, which she had no doubt Mary was waiting for, Carol casually said, "He's going to be here in St. Louis for Thanksgiving visiting family. He wants to meet up. Dinner or...something."

Mary set her cup down and lifted her brows at Carol. "Why do you look so stressed out about that? He seems like a nice boy."

Carol chuckled. "He's almost sixty, Mary. Maybe we can call him a man."

Mary pressed her lips together, clearly not amused by Carol's observation. "Don't you get smart with me, young lady."

Carol's grin widened. "And maybe we should stop calling me young."

Wagging a finger, Mary narrowed her eyes in warning. "Don't try to change the subject."

Looking back into her mug, Carol said, "Yes. He's a nice *man*. And a good friend."

"He wants more?"

Carol shrugged. "I don't know, but I don't want to lead him on if he does."

Mary sprinkled a spoonful of sugar into her coffee. "Why would you be leading him on?"

With her mug almost to her lips, Carol stopped lifting her drink and eyed her mother-in-law. "Because I'm not interested in dating."

"Why not, baby? I think he likes you."

Carol couldn't believe she had to explain this. She watched Mary stir the drink as she stuttered. "I-I'm not... I don't want..."

"A boyfriend?" Mary asked, lifting her coffee. She blew on the drink as she stared at Carol over the rim.

Scoffing, Carol shrugged. "Yeah. I guess that's a way to put it."

"How else would you put it?"

Damn it. She didn't have enough caffeine in her blood to have this conversation. "It doesn't matter because I don't want it."

"Why not?" Mary pressed.

Carol creased her brow. "Because I'm married."

A frown dipped Mary's lips as she set her mug down. An unexpected amount of tension radiated from her.

"I'm *married*," Carol stated again.

"You're clinging to the past like it can save you," Mary said sadly. "It can't, Carol. You ought to know that by now. If anybody ought to know that hanging on to the past isn't healthy, it's you."

Hearing those words from the one person Carol thought would understand stung—not only the implication that she should let go of her marital status but the reminder that

Carol had held on to the anger about Katie's death for too long. "He's only been gone for a year."

"Fourteen months. How long he's been gone doesn't matter. What matters is what we do now."

Carol could count on one hand the times she'd gotten frustrated with Mary over the years. This was about to be one of them. "You think Tobias would want me to throw myself at the first man who came along?"

"I think Tobias would tell you to find a way to be happy again," Mary countered. "He'd want you to pick yourself up and move on."

"I don't need a man for that, Mary."

"No, you don't," Mary stated firmly. "You absolutely do not."

Carol bowed her head slightly. "Thank you."

"But letting that nice man help you through this sure couldn't hurt."

Pushing herself up, Carol snatched the bread off the counter and went to work on unraveling the twist tie. "You know, I am really getting tired of everyone telling me how to grieve for my husband." Adding two slices to the toaster, she pressed the button to turn on the heating elements. "Stop traveling. Get therapy. Go to dinner with Simon. I mean..." Turning, she gawked at Mary. "Why can't you all leave me alone and let me—"

"Shut down and act like this isn't slowly killing you?" Mary asked. She pressed her full lips together, arched a brow, and silently dared Carol to disagree.

"It's too early for this," Carol muttered. "Can I please finish waking up before I get lectured on how to live my life?"

"I'm not telling you how to live your life, but I *am* telling you not to use Tobias as an excuse to not live at all."

The words were like a punch to the gut. Maybe because they were true. Maybe because Carol knew she hung on to the pain because she was so comfortable with it. Hurting was far less scary than letting go. Or maybe she was simply disappointed that no one, not even Mary, seemed to understand her need to find her footing on her own.

"That is not what I'm doing," Carol insisted.

"Finding happiness without Tobias is okay," Mary stated. "Having dinner with Simon or any other man is okay. It's okay for you to live for yourself and not for what could have been."

Carol shook her head again. "I'm not ready for that."

Mary was quiet for a moment before giving one slight nod. "Well, you will be someday. When that day comes, I want you to know I'll support you. I'll still love you. As long as he—whoever *he* is—makes you happy and treats you right, I'll welcome him into this family with open arms."

Carol started to argue, but as the words sank in, she lost the retort she intended to toss out. Mary's words hit on something that Carol hadn't understood until that moment. Despite Lara's lecture the night before insisting that they were a family, Carol hadn't fully understood how terrified she was of losing her spot at their table should she move on.

Without Tobias, they had no reason to let her stay. They had no reason to continue to claim her as their own. This had been the first real family Carol had ever had. Her parents had been cold, and John's parents had been kind, but their marriage had made it impossible for her to ever ingrain herself with them.

The Denmans had given her the first real taste of being part of something bigger. Part of her had been so scared of losing that. Her fear seemed foolish now. She'd never lose Mary, Elijah, or Lara. She'd never stop being Aunt Carol. There would always be a place for her here.

As usual, Mary seemed able to read her thoughts. Her eyes turned sad as she shook her head. "You didn't think we'd turn you out if you moved on, did you?"

Rather than confess, Carol frowned at Mary. "Is this what you and Lara talk about now? My depressing life?"

"Sometimes. Most of the time." Mary grinned and watched Carol for a few long seconds before asking, "Is Simon pushing you?"

Carol shook her head. "Not at all. He's being very supportive. He's never even implied that he wants more. I simply want to quash that idea before he gets his hopes up."

"Seems like he has a lot of respect for you."

The toast popped up, and Carol put a slice of hot bread on two separate plates. After sliding one in front of Mary, she got blackberry jam from the fridge and sat back at the table. "When Aunt Ellen was dishing the dirt back in Ohio, did she happen to mention I had an affair with Simon when I was married to John?"

Mary chuckled. "You know she did."

"He wanted us to get married and raise Katie together. He

went so far as to buy a house and surprise me with the keys. He suggested I quit my job and go back to medical school. He offered me this perfect life that I'd told him over and over I'd given up when I'd married John. One I would never have because John was a drunk and sabotaged every forward step I tried to take."

"Simon loved you back then."

Carol nodded. "I loved him too. I really did. I don't know why I stayed in my miserable life when he gave me a perfect out."

"Because you wanted to do right by Katie," Mary said. "Every decision a mother makes is because she wants to do right by her kids, Carol. You were thinking of Katie."

"I guess." She spread jam onto her toast but dropped the bread back onto the plate, no longer interested in eating it. "Sometimes, I think if I'd married Simon, maybe I'd still have Katie. But that's always followed up with if I'd married Simon, I wouldn't have had Tobias. I get in this tail chase of thoughts. What if this, what if that?"

"Oh, baby," Mary muttered, "you can't pin that on Simon. Your head has worked like that from the day you were born."

Carol closed her eyes and rubbed her forehead. "Nobody knows that better than I do, Mary. Thoughts of Simon exacerbate that, though."

"I don't think that has a damn thing to do with *what if.*" Mary pushed her plate aside as well. "I think you know he wants another chance with you, and part of you wants that too. The other part of you feels guilty because you worry what everyone else will think."

"No." She chuckled. "Not even close. I haven't gotten far enough into the grieving process to even consider having any kind of relationship with anyone. Especially with Simon."

Mary sat back as her eyes filled with questions. "Why do you say that? Why not Simon?"

"He asked me to build a future with him once and I couldn't because I was married. And I can't now because in my heart, I'm married. I can't do that to him twice. That would be cruel."

"Have you told him this?" Mary asked.

Carol shook her head. "No. I don't... I don't even know what he wants. I'm just...doing what I do and creating problems where there aren't any."

"Honey, stop guessing and talk to the man. Have dinner with him when he's in town; tell him what's going on with you."

"Just like that? Just dump my emotional vomit all over him during dinner?"

"Yes. Hell yes. If he can't handle that, then he can't handle being with you anyway."

Carol tilted her head, eyes widened. "What does *that* mean?"

"That means he either accepts that you have broken bits you're trying to fix or he doesn't. Better to know that up front, isn't it?"

Staring at the dark jam soaking into the bread, Carol finally nodded. "Yeah. I need to let him know up front."

"Baby, do you understand that everybody has something? You have Katie and Tobias and, God forgive me for saying this, the aftereffects of being raised by your crazy-ass mother."

Carol chuckled.

"I don't know what Simon has, but I promise you he has something. He has some old wounds that have never healed. He has issues that are going to flare up when you least expect them to. We all have baggage, baby. It's not just you."

"I know," she said softly. "But my baggage seems to be a bit heavier, Mary. Can we drop this now? I would *really* like to enjoy my coffee."

"We'll drop it. As soon as you call him back and let him know you're meeting him."

Cocking a brow at Mary, Carol was ready to defy the order, but the look on her mother-in-law's face was one she'd seen before. Mary wasn't about to let up. With a dramatic groan, Carol unlocked her phone and then called Simon back.

As soon as he answered, she said, "Dinner. Friday night."

"Give him a time," Mary insisted, whispering.

"Six o'clock. You text me where. I'll meet you."

Mary smirked as she sat back. "Good girl."

# FIVE

CAROL SAT on the couch with her youngest niece tucked against her side as they watched floats and marching bands on the television screen. Carol was probably hugging the girl too tight, clinging to the unfiltered affection a little too much, but she knew from seeing the other girls grow, this was probably one of the last parades they'd spend like this.

This tradition used to be Carol, Tobias, and all three of their nieces piled on the sofa oohing and aahing over what came on the screen. Now, Tobias was gone and the two older girls were bored by the parade. Everything was changing so fast. As hard as that was for Carol, she was learning that fighting the changes in her life was futile. Time might seem to drag by sometimes, but it never stopped. Everyone and everything changed, grew. Her tendency to fight those changes was one of the many things impeding her healing.

"Santa," the little one next to her called, pointing at the television.

Carol kissed her head, knowing that as soon as the man on the television disappeared, so would her niece. As expected, within a few minutes, Carol was sitting alone on the couch as the commentators wished their viewers a happy holiday season. Reaching for her phone, she checked her messages, surprisingly disappointed she hadn't heard from Simon yet. That was silly. She'd been the one to subtly set boundaries on their communication since she'd arrived in St. Louis.

Knowing they were going to be in the same town had stirred irrational fear in her. Thanks to Mary's insistence that Carol accept his invitation to dinner, Carol had realized how foolish her response to him had been. Then again, that hadn't a been a reaction to Simon. That'd been in response to Carol's mixed feelings at having him in her life again.

She started to type a text to wish him a happy Thanksgiving but stopped. Just because she was having mixed feelings didn't mean she should be sending him mixed signals. Setting her phone aside, she looked up at the wall of photos Mary had accumulated over the years. She instantly found a photo of her wedding day, which confirmed in her mind that she needed to tread lightly where Simon was concerned. Until she had her head and heart sorted out, she had to be mindful of the signs she was sending to him. Becoming dependent on him to get her through would be too easy, and that wasn't fair to either of them.

Pushing herself up, she walked into the kitchen to join the chaos there. While Lara watched her eldest daughter mixing together ingredients for a casserole, Mary slathered icing onto a cinnamon roll as the other two girls stood by eagerly waiting for a treat. If Tobias were there, he'd be threatening to swipe the rolls and all the icing, causing the girls to protest dramatically. He'd laugh as he teased them until Mary told him to behave himself, despite the smile on her face.

Mary looked up, as if she sensed Carol's gaze on her. Her eyes turned sympathetic, and Carol forced a weak smile, trying to prove that she was fine. She wasn't. Mary clearly knew that. Everyone knew that.

Though this room was filled with the happiness and love that forever lingered, Carol could feel the difference. She felt the underlying emptiness, the sadness that she had been so in tune with, even before burying her husband. She'd felt it all her life, but each loss magnified the feeling a little more.

Carol had the compounded issue of remembering that four years ago, she'd been sitting down to celebrate with her family when her mother had called. In her customary emotionless tone, Judith had shared the news that Carol's father had passed away unexpectedly. Though Carol had never been close to her father, since Tobias's death, she'd been able to work through the old resentments she'd held against her parents.

This was the first Thanksgiving since her father had died that she'd allowed herself to feel the pain of losing him.

Yeah. She was *really* starting to hate holidays. But this feeling was more than that, and thanks to her sessions with Dr. Baxter, Carol had begun see that there was more to her sadness than simply losing her husband unexpectedly. The reality was, she'd had a lifetime of ignoring pain that she could no longer ignore.

All the effort she'd put into pretending that she was okay had made her tired down to her soul.

*Get your head out of that mess.* That was what Tobias would say if he were there, because he'd know where she was going. Rather than focusing on the smiles in front of her, she was looking back. Seeing the sadness. Focusing on the wrong things.

She could no longer deny that her family, friends, and her therapist were right. She had to find a way to move forward. She had to let go not just of Tobias but of all the misery she'd clung to out of fear of leaving the darkness she'd always found comfort in.

She was drawn back to the present when Mary warned the girls about getting icing on the furniture as they ran out of the kitchen, beaming with excitement as they carried their cinnamon rolls with them.

"You know they will," Carol said.

Mary nodded. "They usually do."

"You could tell them they have to eat in the kitchen."

"Grandma's house isn't for setting boundaries," Mary said.

Grinning, Carol walked to Mary and hugged her, partly because she was amused by Mary's logic but mostly because she needed a hug. Mary wrapped her arms around Carol and squeezed tight. Seconds later, Lara joined in, resting her head against Carol's. Though Carol tried to focus on the moment and absorb the love she so desperately needed, there was a part of her that wasn't ready to let go of the pain lingering in the back of her mind.

Tobias's absence was like a thunderstorm brewing. The atmosphere in the home was electrified with the unspoken knowledge that someone was missing. There would be one less chair crammed around the table. One less voice talking over the others.

Lara pulled back from the hug and ran her hand over Carol's back. "How are you doing?"

"I'm okay."

"Liar," she muttered before grabbing two rolls from the plate on the counter and holding one out to Carol.

Carol waved her hand. "Oh, I don't want—"

"Carbs don't count at Mama's house," Lara said.

Her teasing words went through Carol like a hot spear, causing her to jolt as the air was sucked out of her. Those were Tobias's words. That was what he used to tell her when she'd pass on Mary's homemade rolls or cakes. Whenever she'd insisted she was watching what she ate, he'd said, *Carbs don't count at Mama's house.*

One time, when she'd been adamant that she wasn't eating a slice of chocolate cake, Tobias had wrapped his arm around her waist, pinned her against him, and smeared icing over her face. His laughter had rumbled through her, enveloping her in happiness as she squealed in protest. Mary had stormed into the room and lectured Tobias for making a mess, but the smile on her face had betrayed her faux frustration.

They'd had so many moments like that over their time

together. There had been so much laughter and lighthearted teasing. That was one of the tools he'd used to pry her from her shell.

Carol's chest tightened as a voice in the back of her mind reminded her that she'd never have another one like that again. Her lip trembled, and tears filled her eyes. She bit her lip hard, but she was too late. The tsunami of emotions had already hit her. She'd acknowledged the void, she'd faced the pain, and the darkness was now threatening to swallow her whole.

"It's okay, baby," Mary assured her. Rubbing Carol's arm, Mary held her gaze until Carol could blink her tears away. "It's a hard day, but you're okay."

Carol nodded as she accepted the roll Lara held. Easing down at the table, she put the roll on a napkin. Mary and Lara joined her. Though they tried to distract her, Carol's memories were stronger, and she couldn't stop her mind from reliving days that she'd never forget.

———

*Carol tensed as soon as she sat at a table in chemistry class. She had heard snickers from her classmates plenty of times, but she was in no mood for them today. She'd had a long night at the hospital. A stomach virus was going around St. Louis, and she'd spent far too much of her shift holding bedpans for people to vomit into.*

*Most of her classmates were years younger than her. She'd taken time away from her education to work as a nurse and be a wife and mother. Though she wasn't that much older, the difference in maturity was glaring at times. This was one of them.*

*"My God, she smells like bleach and barf," a particularly snotty classmate said. A few people at her table chuckled, but most ignored the comment.*

*Carol opened her mouth, about to tell the little twit to kiss her ass, when a deep voice from the table next to hers spoke up.*

*"Some people don't have everything handed to them," he said. "Some people have to work. Show some respect."*

*Everyone, including Carol, turned to the table. Tobias Denman was staring at the younger woman, clearly not amused by her nasty observation. If this were high school instead of college—which in some ways, these hallways and classrooms were—Tobias would be the cool kid coming to the defense of the nerd. Tobias was the university's football star. Everyone knew him. Carol was a shadow, drifting in and out of classrooms in her scrubs because she never had time to shower and change between work and school. She probably did smell like bleach and vomit, but she didn't care. She wasn't here to make friends or win popularity contests.*

*The younger woman rolled her eyes and scoffed before whispering something to her friends. Carol shook her head. She wasn't going to let someone who acted like that get under her skin. She'd been through a lot worse than schoolyard bullying.*

*By the time the lecture ended and her classmates shuffled from the room like cattle, Carol had already put the confrontation from her mind.*

*At least until Tobias stopped at her table. "You okay?" he asked. His voice rolled through her in an oddly soothing way, like an unexpected lullaby.*

*She grinned as she gathered her books. "You really think her snide comments get to me? I hear worse from my patients before I even start my shift."*

*"You shouldn't have to deal with that kind of shit in the classroom, though. We're all here trying to better ourselves."*

*After stuffing her belongings into her backpack, she hefted the bag strap over one shoulder. "There's always someone who has to cut everybody else down to feel good. I'm the outsider. Makes me an easy target. That's her issue, not mine."*

*He held his hand out. "Tobias Denman."*

*Carol didn't remind him that he was semifamous on campus. Though she didn't attend sporting events, even she knew his name. Tobias Denman, superathlete.*

*Shaking his hand, she introduced herself. Nobody knew her name, which was how she preferred to get through life. Unseen. Unknown. Unbothered. "Carol Bowman."*

*She'd stopped using Caroline when she'd started her new life in St. Louis, but she couldn't bring herself to change her last name—that was the name her daughter had carried for her short life.*

*The warmth of Tobias's hand sent tingles up Carol's arm. He must have felt the strange sensations too, because he looked at their hands as if assessing their connection. She also focused on the hold they had on each other. His large hand engulfed her smaller one. His dark skin made hers seem even more pale than usual. She liked the contrast. Something about the way their skin colors were so different was comforting to her. Yin and yang. Balance.*

*"Are you hungry, Carol? I was about to go grab something to eat. My treat."*

*His question caught her off guard. She stuttered before saying, "You don't have to—"*

*"I want to. My mom's a nurse," he said, as if that explained his reason for offering to feed her. "I know how hard that job is. The stress takes a toll. You shouldn't have to deal with people like that after a long shift. Let me try to make your day better."*

*She gave him a tired smile and gently pulled her hand from his. "Thanks, but you really don't have to. I deal with worse than that every time I walk into the hospital. She doesn't bother me."*

*"Well, she bothers me. I'm not the kind of guy who stands back and watches people get attacked for no reason."*

*"That's a good way to be. The world needs more of that."*

*He suddenly appeared shy. "I have to confess something. I've been trying to figure out a way to ask you out since the semester began. I thought it'd be easier if I came to your rescue. You know, you'd be so filled with gratitude that maybe you'd ask me out instead, but you're kind of blowing off my heroics."*

*Carol's heart did a funny little flip in her chest. He was asking her out? The surge of excitement quickly fizzled and caution creeped in. That old familiar need to look for ulterior motives sparked to life. Her shell was trying to close, to shut him out before he got too close and he had the ability to hurt her.*

*Tilting her head, Carol asked, "Do I look like I need to be rescued?"*

"Actually," he said softly, as if he was about to profess something else, "you look like you need a friend. You're sad," Tobias continued when she didn't respond. "I can sense that about you. I have from the first time you walked into this classroom. Somebody hurt you. What happened?"

His words touched something unexpected. Her need to pull away halted. She was so good at hiding that she was shocked he'd seen her. If Carol was good at anything, it was blending into the background. Going unnoticed was so much easier. Not physically. Of course people saw her—she wasn't invisible. But she could hide her feelings, her emotions, so well that she prevented anyone from connecting with her. From seeing her. But Tobias had seen through her, and he had the gall to tell her what he'd seen.

Carol pushed thoughts of Katie away before the words slipped from her lips. Before she told this stranger that her daughter had died. That she'd left her husband who had drank too much too often. That her life was one empty day after another and she had no idea what the future held. That the only reason she'd registered to get her master's degree was because the only part of her that continued to make sense was her desire to be more than she was. All she had left of her former self was the ambition instilled in her as a child.

Every day of her life was the same as the one before, and she was tired. She was tired and lost, and yes, she needed a friend.

Instead of saying any of that, she smirked. "If you got vomited on for a living, you'd be sad too."

He laughed, and like magic, some of the pain in her soul eased. There was a light about him, calling her to him. The only *other time in her life she'd experienced an instant connection like that was when she'd met John. However, John's gravitational pull had been laden with warning signs that Carol had chosen to overlook.*

*She didn't feel that sense of danger coming from Tobias. She was at peace. Calm. She was centered as he stared at her. When was the last time she'd felt centered? Had she ever?*

*"I am hungry," she said, despite her brain telling her to run from this man before he could peel back her carefully constructed layers. She shut out the logic and listened to her heart. For once, she was going to trust her instincts and see where she ended up. "Let's get something to eat."*

*A bright smile spread across Tobias's face. "Now you're talking."*

---

As soon as Carol answered the incoming call on her cell phone, her mother asked, "Why do you sound so tired?"

Sitting at Mary's kitchen table, Carol eyed the slice of pumpkin pie she'd served. She didn't know why she'd gotten another slice. She'd already eaten pie. Something about Thanksgiving made indulgence appealing, but she didn't have any more of an appetite now than she had earlier in the day.

"It's been a long day," Carol said.

"What happened?"

Carol smirked. "Thanksgiving happened, Mom. Cooking,

cleaning, a houseful of people. I sound tired because I *am* tired. It's been a *long* day," she said again.

Judith was quiet, likely scowling on the other end of the call, but one of the things her mother had been working on was thinking before speaking. She'd learned that saying the first thing that came to mind wasn't necessarily beneficial to the progress they had made in their relationship.

"How was your day?" Carol asked.

"Terrible. Instead of cooking here, Ellen convinced me to go to the community center to get a meal there. The turkey was dry, the potatoes were cold, and the rolls were so hard they could have hurt someone. The pie was obviously one of those cheap things you buy in the freezer section. I think the gravy came out of a jar. We won't be doing that again."

"It was fine," Ellen said in the background.

"It was not," Judith countered. "The turkey was dry."

"We got to eat with our neighbors. It was fine."

Carol smiled as she clearly pictured the two women bickering. "I'll be there to help with Christmas dinner. We'll make a turkey and homemade pie then, Mom."

"How soon will you be here?"

"I need to reserve a spot for the RV, so I'm not sure. Next week probably."

Judith was quiet for several seconds before saying, "It would be nice if you could give me some warning."

"I will."

"I need to make sure your aunt has time to clean up that mess she leaves in the spare room."

"It's her studio, Mom," Carol said. "She's allowed to leave a mess in her studio."

"It's a disaster. I don't know how she finds anything in there."

She was tempted to tell her mom she was living in an RV, that Aunt Ellen didn't need to clean up her studio to make room. However, Carol was done having that conversation. The last time she'd visited, her mother nearly had a fit until Carol agreed to sleep on the uncomfortable sofa in her aunt's art room. She was convinced that sleeping at a campground wasn't safe.

"I'll call Monday to make a reservation," Carol said. "I'll let you know when to expect me."

"Thank you." Another stretch of silence filled the line. "How is therapy going?"

Carol rolled her eyes. "Fine."

"You always say that."

Pushing her plate away, Carol sat back and frowned. "Because saying anything more than that is too personal, Mom."

"Too personal? I'm your mother."

Carol almost laughed. That was the point. One of the many issues Carol was working through was her childhood. Though she and her mother were on even ground now, that didn't mean a lifetime of Judith Stewart hadn't left a mark on Carol's psyche. "That doesn't mean I'm going to share my counseling sessions with you."

"I'm not asking you to..."

Ellen mumbled something in the background that Carol

couldn't make out, but whatever she'd said was enough to get her mother to stop pressing. Thank goodness for Aunt Ellen.

"What did you do today," Carol asked, redirecting her mother's attention, "besides eat bad food?"

As her mother ran down her day, Carol threw away the pie she hadn't eaten and put her dish in the sink to be added to the dishwasher once the current load finished running. Hearing the distinctive beep of someone else calling her line, Carol pulled the phone from her ear. Like the savior she tended to be, Alyssa's name appeared on the screen.

"Mom," Carol said, "I've got another call coming in that I need to take. I'll call you back tomorrow."

Judith sighed, so Carol quickly added, "It's a friend. We're working on plans for meeting up." That wasn't exactly a lie. Alyssa had been trying to talk Carol into heading back to Houston for at least a visit since the day Carol had left.

"Okay," Judith said, sounding less offended. "Okay. I'm glad you're getting out and seeing people. That's important. Good night."

"Night, Mom. Love you." She barely heard her mother respond in kind before connecting to Alyssa's call. "I don't know why you're calling, but *thank you*."

She chuckled. "Saving you from your mother?"

"*Saving* is not quite accurate, but close enough that we don't have to search for another way to put it." Walking out the back door, Carol sat on the stairs before asking, "How was your day?"

Alyssa didn't answer, and Carol's smile faded. Clearly Alyssa probably wasn't just calling to check on her. Alyssa and her husband had been having problems for several months now. Longer, really, but only recently had it seemed things were coming to a head. "What happened, Lys?"

"Jason and I had a fight on the way home from his mom's house after dinner. He's going to move out for a while."

Carol closed her eyes and did her best to hold in the sigh that wanted to leave her. She hated when her mother exhaled those long, disappointing breaths. She wasn't going to do that to her friend. She'd had so many talks with Alyssa about her marital problems that she wasn't surprised, but she'd hoped they could work things out. "I'm sorry."

"I get why this is so hard for you now. I'm not a widow but...the idea of my husband not being here every day..."

"I know," Carol said. "That's difficult."

Alyssa sniffled, and Carol wished she could hug her friend. If she were in Houston, they'd be sitting on Carol's couch sipping wine as they consoled each other.

"Tell me you're coming home soon," Alyssa said softly. "I need you right now."

Carol looked up at the sky. The city lights weren't visible from Mary's backyard but were bright enough to block out the stars. The barely illuminated sky seemed fitting. "I'm spending Christmas with Mom," Carol said. "Then I'll swing through Houston."

"Swing through?" Alyssa asked, sounding like she was about to cry. "Carol. *Please*. We both know where this is headed. I'm going to get divorced."

Carol closed her eyes when Alyssa's voice cracked. The one and only time Carol had ever been asked to be a matron of honor was at Alyssa's wedding. Her friend had only been married nine years. Not nearly long enough to give up. "You don't know that."

"I do. I've known that for a long time. I've been telling you for months. He doesn't love me anymore."

"You—" Carol stopped herself from telling Alyssa she had to try harder, talk more, be more present. She'd been on the receiving end of unwanted advice since Tobias had died. She didn't want to do that to her friend. "He loves you, Lys. Even if things have gotten bad, he still loves you. He always will."

Alyssa let out a soft crying sound.

"I'm here for you," Carol said softly, "but I don't know if I can come back to Houston to stay. Being in St. Louis is hard enough, and we haven't lived here for years. Being in Houston without Tobias... I'm not sure I can do that."

"I know," Alyssa said. "I'm being selfish."

Carol smiled. "No, I'm honored that you need me. I'm just not in a good place either." Rather than let the conversation dissolve into analyzing Carol's problems, she said, "Tell me what happened. Why were you fighting?"

As she listened, Carol thought how she'd give anything if her biggest problem this holiday season was not feeling heard by her spouse. She'd give anything if Tobias was simply fed up with her bad habits instead of lying in a grave a few miles away.

Though she wanted to remind Alyssa how lucky she was that Jason was there to work through their problems, Carol kept that bit of wisdom to herself.

# SIX

CAROL FROWNED and shook her head at the sweater Lara held up. The little boutique was crammed full of people bumping into one another, rushing to get merchandise before the shelves ran out of the size, color, or design they wanted. Carol didn't usually mind these types of scenes, but she hadn't been sleeping well and would have preferred to stay at Mary's, sitting on the sofa reading a book that had nothing to do with the holidays.

"You're making this difficult," Lara muttered as she carelessly refolded the sweater and dropped the wool onto the shelf.

"In what world would that color look good on me?"

Lara eyed the mustard yellow–dyed wool and then Carol. "So, pick something else. Mary wants to buy you a *nice, warm* sweater."

"I don't need—"

"I don't care," Lara stated, cutting her off. "Mary told me

to buy you a sweater for her to give you for Christmas. Pick out a damn sweater so we can get out of this madhouse."

"You dragged me here," Carol grumbled as she grabbed a black cable knit off the shelf. She checked the size, scanned for any imperfections, and then handed the shirt to Lara. "I don't know why you do this to us every year. We both hate the crowds."

"Because the sales are good," Lara said, adding the sweater to the ever-growing pile over her arm.

"There are good sales all the way through January," Carol said.

"But Black Friday sales are better."

Carol shook her head. "Marketing makes you think that, but it's not true."

"It *is* true. Besides, you spent over an hour picking over every shelf at the toy store, so don't lecture me about taking too long."

Frowning, Carol said, "I was shopping for *your* girls."

"My girls don't need all that crap you bought."

Carol blew a raspberry. "Whatever. My job, as their aunt, is to spoil them."

Lara frowned as she turned to another display and sorted through the pile of disheveled clothes. Though there were associates on the floor, they couldn't keep up with the disarray the herd of customers was leaving in their wake. "Spoiling them would be a lot easier if you came back to St. Louis."

Carol glared. "Don't use those sweet girls against me, Lara. That's too low. Even for you."

Smirking, Lara shook her head and turned toward the line to check out. Neither spoke as they waited their turn. Carol sensed Lara was plotting her next attempt at getting her way, so Carol reminded herself of all the reasons she'd decided to live on the road for the foreseeable future.

She needed to regain her independence. She wanted to honor Tobias by seeing places he hadn't seen. Being alone gave her time to think without everyone else invading her thoughts. The quiet of the evening didn't seem quite so bad in the confines of the RV.

As they were headed back toward Lara's SUV, already half-filled with shopping bags, Lara said, "You could move in with us. I'll need your help if I get this promotion. My job will be more demanding. Adjusting to the demands could be hard for all of us. The girls would love having you live with us."

Carol gawked at her sister-in-law, gauging how serious she was in the offer. She seemed serious enough. "I'm not moving in with you," Carol said.

Lara pushed the button on her remote to lift the tailgate on her SUV. After they stuffed their bags in, Lara slammed the door shut again. She turned to Carol, but before she could speak, Carol shook her head.

"Stop it, Lara. I meant it."

"Stop worrying about you?"

"Stop trying to force me to move on in the way that is most comfortable for you."

"You aren't moving on. That's the problem."

"That's your perception," Carol snapped. "I have been to

hell and back in the last year, and I am so done without people telling me how I should be handling that. My daughter is dead. My husband is dead."

Lara jolted as if surprised that she'd finally pushed Carol's last button. Her mouth opened like she wanted to say something, but she didn't utter a word.

"I know you lost Tobias too," Carol continued with a strained voice, "but he was *my* husband. *My* rock. It was *my* day-to-day life that was turned upside down. You get to go about your routines, your work, your hobbies, and only think about him sometimes. Only be reminded of him *sometimes*. I wake up every morning an empty bed and the reminder that he's gone. Every goddamn day, Lara. You don't get to tell me how to make that better."

"That's not what I'm..." She let her words trail off when Carol challenged her with the lift of a brow.

"You're acting like my mother. Trying to force me to live the life that suits you and to hell with what I want. You just keep pushing and pushing without hearing a word I say to you. Like you somehow know what's best for me."

"Damn it," Lara muttered after a few tense seconds. "You're right. I *am* acting like your mother. I'm sorry."

The edge of Carol's anger softened. "I know you're worried, but I'll be okay," she said. "I haven't figured out how yet. But that's not something that moving to St. Louis is going to fix. I need time, and I need space. I need my sister to understand that."

"I'm trying," Lara said. "I really am. You can't blame me for being scared that we're going to lose you too."

Carol considered Lara's statement for a moment. "Do you think I'm going to hurt myself? Is that what this is about?"

Lara didn't answer, but the concern on her face confirmed her fears.

"Jesus, Lara. I'm not that far gone."

"Like you said," Lara whispered, "you've been to hell and back in the last year. You've had a lot thrown at you with John resurfacing and bringing up all that stuff with Katie. What if you hit a low and you're by yourself? You might think that's the way out."

Carol shook her head. "Is Mary worried about this too?"

"She hasn't said as much."

Leaning against the SUV, Carol scanned the parking lot as she processed what Lara had said. "If losing Katie taught me anything, it's that life goes on despite the pain. I found a really good life with Tobias. And someday, when I'm ready, I'll find a good life again." She returned her focus to Lara. "But you and Mary and my mother can't decide when, where, or how that happens. Only I can decide that."

"I know."

"I don't think you do know," Carol stated. "You have to stop pressuring me. I have enough to deal with already. I can't worry about living up to your expectations. I can't spend my time tiptoeing around your concerns when I'm trying to find my footing. Do you understand that? Do you understand how unfair that is?"

Lara was quiet for several long seconds before nodding. "Yeah. I'm sorry."

"Back off and let me work this out on my own, okay?"

"Okay." Opening her arms, Lara hugged Carol tight. "I really am sorry. I love you."

"I love you too." Pulling back, Carol peered up as a dark gray cloud closed in on the sun. Though there weren't calls for rain in the forecast, the sky told a different story. She'd guess they were in for sprinkles at the very least. The weather seemed fitting for her mood.

Now that she wasn't ignoring the darkness looming so close to the surface, she had to admit that she could understand Lara's concerns. As hard as Carol tried to hide behind the facade she used as armor, those closest to her were seeing the cracks. In a sense, Carol thought she should be thankful, but she still wasn't used to relying on anyone other than Tobias to see her through times like these.

As soon as they climbed into the SUV, Carol buckled in and forced herself to open up and voice something that had been bothering her. "Being on the road made so much more sense when I promised John that I wouldn't fall back into autopilot." She scoffed at the irony. "Can you believe after twenty-four years, I let that idiot talk me into something stupid?"

Lara glanced at her. "You were looking for meaning, and he gave you some. Living your life to the fullest on the road made sense."

"Nothing makes sense without Tobias. I understand that's a temporary feeling and someday I'll find my way again, but..." Carol frowned as she stared out the passenger window. "After Katie, I was able to find a path to move forward. Living again wasn't easy, but I found a way. I was able to put one foot in front of the other. Losing Tobias..."

"You're right," Lara said. "You're still finding your footing. I'm sorry if I made that more difficult for you."

Carol shook her head slightly. "He would want me to move on and be happy. I don't know what that means yet."

"Maybe Simon could help you figure that out," Lara said tentatively.

"Maybe," Carol said. "Maybe Simon will factor into that *someday*. But I'm not ready to think about opening my heart up and starting something I can't finish. It wouldn't be fair to Simon. I did that to him once already. He deserves better than that. I'm not going to hurt him again."

"I understand that," Lara said. "But you have to admit, you could do worse."

Carol chuckled as Simon's face flashed through her mind. "Yeah, I could do a lot worse."

"Please don't ever feel like you're alone. You're not. You're never alone." Lara grabbed Carol's hand. "We're family. No matter what."

"No matter what," Carol agreed.

———

*Caroline let out a quiet sigh as Simon walked into the coffee shop where they often met. She wasn't ready to say what she had to tell him, but the train they were on had been on the wrong tracks from the start. She had to put an end to the ride before the inevitable disaster.*

*As he sat across from her and gave her a weak greeting, she sensed he understood why she'd summoned him.*

*A week ago, he'd pulled her into a stairwell at the hospital and handed her a key to his new house. Or, as he'd called it, their* new house. *He'd done what she'd been dreading from the day they'd given in to their desires. He'd asked her to leave her husband so they could start a life together. Not just a life for her and Simon but for Katie too.*

*If not for Katie, Caroline would have jumped at the chance. Katie was such a happy girl. A daddy's girl. Their daughter seemed to sense the underlying dysfunction within John, and her caring nature—the nature she'd inherited from Caroline—made her want to fix what was wrong. If anyone could help John see how far he'd fallen into the abyss of alcoholism, that person would be Katie.*

*Those two were closer than peas in a pod. Katie was the center of John's world, and as much as Caroline hated to admit, John was the center of Katie's. Over the last week, considering the impact a divorce would have on them had made Caroline realize how selfish she would be to tear their lives apart.*

*"You don't have to say it," Simon said softly as silence lingered between them. "I knew I was risking pushing you away when I asked you to move in with me. That was a risk I had to take."*

*"I wish I could be that brave," Caroline said, her voice thin from the lack of confidence she had in her decision.*

*She'd told John that she was considering a divorce. She hadn't told him why, but she had a thousand reasons and he knew that. He hadn't even asked for a reason. He'd begged her to stay. He'd promised to stop drinking and to be more responsible. He'd even suggested that once Katie started school in the fall, Caroline could do what she'd wanted for so long and go to medical school.*

*Simon had offered her that as well. Caroline knew Simon would follow through. She knew he'd stand by her and support her. She knew he'd be there for her and Katie.*

*She also knew that John would likely stumble and fall and leave her empty-handed as he'd done so many times over the course of their marriage. But for some reason, she couldn't leave him. She couldn't tear apart the family she'd worked so hard to keep together.*

*Simon was everything Caroline had ever wanted. But John needed her. Katie needed her parents together. How could Caroline choose her own happiness over that of her child? How could she look Katie in the eye and tell her they were going to live someplace where her daddy couldn't be?*

*Tears filled Caroline's eyes, and she bit her lip hard in an attempt to keep her emotions at bay. "I have to think of Katie first."*

*Simon nodded. "She'd be happy, Caroline. We'd give her the stable life that she deserves."*

*"I know, but...John is her father. She needs him."*

*"What do you need?" Simon asked.*

*Caroline turned her face away before she started crying. When she thought she could speak without breaking, she calmly said, "I need to give my daughter the best chance at having a happy life that I can give her." Finding the strength to look at*

*Simon again, Caroline added, "I can't rip her world apart just because John pisses me off."*

*"John is holding you back, and by holding you back, he's holding Katie back. Children recover from divorce. Sometimes they actually thrive after being removed from a negative environment. You know, one where the parents are constantly fighting because one of them is a drunk."*

*His words caused her breath to catch. Mostly because he was right, but damn him for speaking that truth right now.*

*"We're going to fix this," she said. Even she didn't believe the words. Things had been great between her and John for the last two days. She'd slapped him with a reality check. He'd gotten rid of all the beer in the house, helped her clean, and had even been somewhat pleasant to be around. To top it all off, he'd suggested the time had come for her to go back to school. He'd promised to be more helpful and supportive so she could finally become a pediatrician.*

*Caroline knew from far too much experience that this change in her husband wouldn't last. So, while they would be better for a while, they wouldn't be fixing anything. They'd be healing just enough that they didn't break. She understood their cycle better now. But she had to try. For Katie. She had to do her best for her daughter.*

*Simon frowned as he sat back. "I wish I could be mad, but I have no right to be. I'm asking you to end your marriage and you're saying no. I should be furious because I'm the better man for you, but I don't have the right."*

*Caroline closed her eyes as tears threatened to spill. "You can* be mad. I never should have... I'm the bad guy here, Simon. Not you. Not even John. Not this time. This time, I'm the culprit."

"Christ, Caroline," he said, sounding desperate. "You deserve more. Why can't you see you deserve more?"

Furrowing her brow, she looked across the table at him. "This isn't about me, Simon. I have a child to raise. I have a little girl who thinks her father hung the moon. I can't hurt her to make my life easier. I won't."

"I get that. I really do." He dragged his hand over his face. They'd both worked a long shift, and the tension between them had been escalating all week. As Caroline came to accept that this moment was imminent, she'd done her best to avoid him in the corridors so he couldn't corner her. No doubt he was as exhausted as she was.

Usually, in a moment like this, she'd reach out and touch him. Give him a bit of comfort with their intimate contact and sweet smiles. She couldn't do that now, and she was already missing the feel of him. Those secret moments gave her as much strength as they'd given to him.

"I don't resent you for choosing Katie over me," he said. "I never would, but I'm going to tell you right now, you're going to regret this." He didn't say the words out of anger. His eyes were sad, his voice subdued. He wasn't threatening her with the outcome they both knew would happen; he was pleading with her. "You're not protecting Katie," he said. "You may think you are, but you aren't. She sees you suffering, Caroline. She's learning this is what marriage is supposed to be. You're teaching her that what he is doing is okay. You aren't protecting her.

*When you realize that, let me know. I'll be there to help you pick up the pieces."*

*Caroline's heart dropped to her stomach as he stood. Leaning over, he put a gentle kiss to her forehead. Tears fell down her cheeks as she tightened her hands into fists so she didn't grab him. The urge to cling to him, to tell him she was wrong—she already knew she was wrong—and beg for forgiveness for even thinking of ending their affair was so strong, she could barely control it.*

*"I love you," he whispered before walking away.*

*She very nearly called out to him and asked him to come back, to talk her out of going back to John, but she didn't. She'd made her choice. She'd closed the door on the life she so desperately wanted, but she'd done so for Katie. That was the one thing she had to hold on to. She'd made the right choice for Katie. So long as she could see her little girl's smile, Caroline could get through anything. Even losing the man she was so desperately in love with.*

———

Carol walked into the steakhouse where she was meeting Simon. Her stomach fluttered nervously when she spotted him sitting on a bench in the entryway. He smiled the moment he noticed her, and she couldn't help but smile as well. His beard was trimmed short, and his gray hair appeared freshly cut. Clearly he'd taken his break from the hospital to do a little self-care. She was glad. He'd been sounding far too stressed lately.

He stood and met her with open arms, which she slipped into without hesitation. She closed her eyes as he squeezed her against him and held on until he eased his hold. She probably would have held on indefinitely. Even though she'd struggled to commit to this dinner, seeing him in person eased more than just her nerves. As always, he had a calming presence that soothed her mind. While she'd never readily admit how much she appreciated his hug, she couldn't ignore that once again, just being with him gave her that sense of peace she'd been missing.

He had a way of grounding her. "Did you have a good Thanksgiving?" he asked as he gripped her hands. Though his question was generic, the depth of concern in his eyes was obvious. He wasn't asking about her meal or time spent with family. He was asking how she'd coped spending the holiday as a widow.

"I had a good day," she said. That wasn't a complete lie. Despite the shadow of Tobias's loss looming over the dinner table, Carol had been able to stay in the present and enjoy being with her family. "How was yours?"

"I lost fifty bucks to my brother on a football game, but other than that, it was pretty good," he said before gesturing toward the hostess, who was patiently standing by with two menus.

Carol followed the young woman to a booth. Simon sat across from her, and Carol couldn't deny the serenity of being there with him. She'd expected the dinner to be awkward, but she should have known better. She could count on one hand the times she was unsettled around

Simon—most of those were the times they got locked into an intense staring contest leading up to the start of their affair.

Like Tobias, there was a calm about Simon that embraced her, soothing her chaotic mind.

"I'm glad you had a good Thanksgiving," Simon said as they settled at the table.

"Well, I admit there were a few moments where I struggled. Sometimes things sneak up and pull the rug out from under me. Being with Tobias's family made it better."

"I'm sure having them rally around you is nice."

Carol tilted her head as she considered how to answer. Though she and Lara had made peace, she couldn't discount how her sister-in-law was so determined to get Carol to come back to St. Louis. "In one sense, yes. In another..."

"They're suffocating you."

She scoffed. "That sounds so ungrateful."

"It doesn't," Simon countered.

"It does, and I am aware of that. They love me and want to help, but they can't go through the grieving process for me."

"No, they can't."

She glanced around the restaurant. "They want me to move back to St. Louis, but if I did, I'd let them push me into moving on the way they want me to. I need to find out what my life is now without worrying about what that means to anyone else." She realized he likely thought she'd looped him into that. Perhaps she had without intending to, because one of the things weighing on her the last few weeks was worrying that she couldn't fill the role he might want her to fill.

Their conversation was interrupted by their waiter. They both requested sweet tea and then placed their orders. When their waiter disappeared, Simon rested his crossed arms on the table and stared at Carol with the same intensity that had shaken her all those years ago. Though his light brown eyes didn't have quite the same impact as when she was stuck in a sad and lonely marriage, she couldn't deny he comforted her soul simply by being there.

Warmth filled Carol's cheeks when she caught herself getting lost in his gaze like she used to. "I want to be upfront about something."

He grinned. "This isn't a date."

She laughed lightly. "No, it's not."

"I wasn't trying to put our time together into that context."

"Even so," she said, "I need you to know that I'm in a weird place right now, Simon. John showing up out of nowhere over the summer forced me to face a lot of things. This is more than just losing Tobias. I'm finally allowing myself to heal from losing Katie. I held on to that pain for a long time because I didn't want to face how much it hurt. I don't want you to feel like you have to save me again. You don't. Even with Tobias's loss, I'm stronger now than I was back then."

"I'm not trying to save you," Simon gently said. "I just wanted to have dinner with you."

She smiled when he gave her a teasing grin. "Me too," she

said, "but I also want to be honest with you." She glanced around at other diners, trying to find the right words. "I regretted that I let us get to a place where you..." Shaking her head, she forced herself to look at him. "I shouldn't have let things go so far that you invested so much into a future I couldn't give to you."

"That was my choice," he said. "I knew you were in a bad place with John back then, and I know you're grieving Tobias now. I'm not trying to pressure you into anything, Caroline. I apologize if it came across that way."

"It didn't. But...we've been talking a lot lately, and I don't want—"

"You don't want me to get the wrong idea of where this is headed," he said, finishing her sentence.

Embarrassment settled over her. "Yeah. *That.*" Carol gnawed at the inside of her lip as their waiter put their drinks on the table and let them know their meals would be ready soon.

Once they were alone, Simon took a drink and then placed his glass aside. "I care about you," he said. "Even when we lost contact for all those years, I wished you well. Now that our paths have crossed again, I'm enjoying getting to know who you are now. Maybe, someday, we can see if that takes us somewhere else, but for now"—he shrugged—"let's enjoy where we are."

Carol considered his suggestion before nodding. "I hate how you always say the right thing."

His lips spread into a brilliant smile. "I can honestly think of worse traits for you to hate than that."

"Like?" she asked, glad he was changing the subject.

He groaned as he sat back. "I'm terrible at recycling. I'd rather toss a can than clean the thing out and separate it into the right bin. I just rinse the jars and cans, toss everything into one container, and let someone else sort through them later."

Carol reared back as if he'd said something unfathomable. Pressing her hand to her chest, she widened her eyes at him. "How could you?"

He lifted his hands as if he couldn't explain himself. "I also wear my shoes in the house, which, according to my ex-wife, was why we couldn't have nice things."

Carol laughed and then, without thinking, asked, "What was she like?"

"My ex-wife? Too good for me. She was patient and kind. A wonderful mother. She wanted me to open a specialty clinic so I could have more normal hours and be more involved with her and our girls. I couldn't do it," he confessed. "I don't know why I couldn't do it. The crazy hours at the hospital were destroying our marriage. I knew that, but I couldn't give up the job."

"Because your job was important," Carol said.

"Because being in the mix of things was addicting," he countered. "You know as well as I do how the rush, the excitement, the unexpected gets under your skin. You don't have that in a clinic. Clinics are calm, organized. Boring."

Carol shook her head. "That might have been part of it, but the biggest part was knowing you played a vital role in the care of those children. The hours were crazy, the job was draining, but what you did was important. And you knew that. You were brilliant at what you did, Simon."

She wasn't simply blowing smoke to make him feel better. The thing that had stuck out to her all those years ago was the compassion he had for his patients. He was an amazing pediatric pulmonologist. He'd been considered one of the best in the region for a reason.

"So were you," he said softly. "I wish..." He glanced away and pressed his lips tightly together. He didn't finish, but he didn't have to. They'd talked so many times about how wonderful their lives would be once she went back to school and became a pediatrician like she'd planned. How exciting their careers would be once they were working together in that capacity. They'd had big plans. Plans she'd walked away from.

"I couldn't stay," she said. That was all she had to say. He'd been there the night she'd reached her breaking point. He'd held her as she cried over the loss of her daughter. He'd seen how utterly destroyed she was.

"You found the place you needed to be," he said. "The family you needed to help you heal. I'm happy for you. But that doesn't mean I don't wish things had been different."

"I think about that sometimes. But if things had been different, you wouldn't have your daughters. You wouldn't change a thing, Simon."

"I would change *one* thing," he said as he gently gripped her hand, and she knew he meant Katie.

She gave him a sad smile. "Yeah. One."

"But we can't," he continued, pulling his hand away, "and now you're a vagabond and I'm a lackluster chief of staff."

"*Lackluster*?" she asked, following his lead in once again changing the subject. "I doubt that."

He shrugged. "Maybe, maybe not. But that doesn't matter anymore."

"Why?"

"Because I'm going to quit," he stated.

Carol lifted her brows, stunned by his announcement. "What... Why?"

"I've decided to retire."

"Since when?"

"Since I've had a few days away to think." He winked at her. "I've been inspired to travel."

Carol shook her head. "Oh, no. Don't you put this insanity off on me. You're burned out. That's not my fault."

"I'm *so* burned out," he admitted. "I bought some acreage down south a few years ago and built a house surrounded by nothing but trees and wildlife. Being there is so peaceful. I swear, I can actually hear myself think when I'm there. I don't have a million voices running through my mind, demanding to be heard. I used to go there a few times a year to get away, but I want to be there permanently. I want to surround myself with that kind of quiet so I can rest now."

"Sounds amazing."

"Have you rested yet?" he asked, and that hint of concern returned to his eyes. He might have been treading more lightly, but he clearly was as worried as Lara, Mary, and the rest of Carol's family.

Carol swallowed before shaking her head. "Not yet, but I'm getting burned out too," she admitted. "Only in a different way. I've been trying so hard to find the right way to honor Tobias, and I just... I can't seem to get it right, you know? But I'm tired too."

"Maybe you can visit me there sometime. I bet you'll find the same kind of peace there that I have."

He pulled his phone from his pocket and, after a few taps and swipes, turned the screen so she could see the retreat for herself. A wraparound porch hugged a two-story log house with so many windows, the views would be visible no matter where someone was inside.

Carol had fallen in love with the Ozarks when she and Tobias had honeymooned at a cabin close to trails to hike and caves to explore. The mountains and forests provided the type of adventures Carol preferred. She and Tobias had even tried their hands at rock climbing. They'd often talked about buying land in the area and building a getaway, much like the one Simon was showing her now. That was one of the many things she and her husband had put off doing for another time. Neither acknowledging, until it was too late, that maybe they wouldn't have time.

Simon swiped to another photo. "See that? Hiking for miles without another person in sight. It's perfect."

A little twinge of jealousy struck her. She would love to have a place like that. Maybe when she finally decided she was ready to settle down, she'd try to find a few acres too. Sitting back, she chuckled. "Remember when I told you about that woman I met in Utah? She didn't want to hike by herself in case she fell and needed help. You might want to take that into consideration before wandering into those woods alone."

"Nah. Survival of the fittest." His smile spread as he changed the image. "This is the view from the back porch. Isn't that amazing?"

The house sat high enough on a peak that the deck overlooked an endless forest covering rolling hills. Though the picture was taken when the trees were filled with lush, green leaves, Carol pictured how they'd appear when the colors would be vibrant reds, yellows, and oranges.

"Wow," she whispered.

Simon turned the screen to admire the photo himself. "Imagine staring out at that with your morning coffee."

"That's amazing, Simon. I'm so happy for you. You're going to love being there."

His face sagged the slightest bit. "Yeah. I'll love being there more when I can get my kids to agree to visit me. Apparently, there's not enough to keep them entertained. Being in the mountains is boring, they say. And by boring, they mean not enough restaurants and clubs and—"

"Internet speed."

He pointed his finger at her. "Bingo. That's the real problem."

She laughed. "That can be fixed."

Setting his phone aside, he said, "I like the quiet. Most of the time. I have to admit, though, sometimes after a long day, I miss having someone to talk to." He grinned, looking a bit shy as he glanced at her. "I guess that's why I've been harassing you so much these days. Chatting with you about my day is nice."

"It is," Carol agreed. "Although, I confess, I just appreciate having someone who isn't so vocal about their concerns for my welfare."

"I'm concerned," Simon countered. "But I also respect that you're an adult who can figure things out on her own."

"Oh. Well"—she toasted him with her tea—"I appreciate that too. You're in a very small, select group of people. I think I got the point across to my sister-in-law today, but I'll never convince most of my family."

Simon's eyes shifted back to having a depth of concern. "You do understand why they're worried, don't you?"

She focused on her glass, taking a moment to measure her words before meeting his gaze again. "Any discussion about my mental, physical, or emotional health is off the table. Okay? I have a therapist and an overbearing mother for those conversations."

He also took a moment. "Okay. Fair enough."

"Thank you."

Sitting back, he asked, "So, will you?"

Carol cocked a brow at him. "Will I what?"

"Visit me in the Ozarks? You can stay for as long as you want." He chuckled when she simply stared at him. "There's that dreaded silence again. You really have to learn to say no, Caroline."

"And you have to learn to quit throwing these crazy ideas at me out of nowhere."

"You used to like my crazy ideas."

She opened her mouth, ready to counter, but then snapped her lips shut as she recalled how intensely passionate—and, yes, *crazy*—their short affair had been. They'd taken a lot of risks that could have cost them both, more than they'd understood or allowed themselves to consider. "I was younger then."

Simon laughed heartily, making her smile.

"Can I tell you a secret?" he asked as his amusement faded.

She hesitated, not sure she wanted to hear what he had to say, but curiosity won out. "Yeah. Tell me a secret."

"The thing I missed most after you left was our talks. Don't get me wrong, the rest was amazing," he said, causing Carol to blush, "but I've never had such deep and honest conversations with anyone else. Not even my ex-wife. I miss that."

She understood exactly what he meant. Their relationship had been more than stolen kisses, flirty looks, and passionate sex. They'd related on a level much deeper than a simple physical connection. They'd shared an intellectual bond that she'd never had before.

Simon may not have found another partner to share those moments with, but she'd managed to find a similar bond with Tobias. They'd spend hours delving deep into a topic, pulling things apart to better understand them. That kind of intimacy was underrated by a lot of people, which had made their connection even that much more special to her. The rarity of what she'd had with Tobias provided such a strong bond between them. That was likely why she felt such a bond with Simon, even though they hadn't seen each other for decades until a few months before.

Simon had said something that suddenly shone a light on the one thing she couldn't figure out. Of course she missed her husband, of course she missed the life they'd built over the years, but suddenly, she understood the part of her grief she hadn't been able to name before. She still had people to talk to. She was never without someone to call or someone calling her. What was missing was the depth Tobias had brought to their conversations. The exchanges she had now didn't come close to reaching the depth she'd had with Tobias.

That she'd once had with Simon.

And *that* was the piece of her life that she'd been missing since losing her husband.

Understanding dawned on her like the sun finally breaking through the clouds as a storm dispersed. The sudden clarity took her breath away.

"Here we go," their server said, disturbing the soul-baring moment that Simon had unwittingly instigated.

Carol blinked back to the present as a steak and a heaping pile of steamed vegetables were set in front of her. She smiled her thanks and waited for the young man to leave before looking across the table.

"I said the wrong thing again," Simon commented once they were alone.

"Actually," she said, "I think you said exactly what I've been needing to hear."

"I'm going to have to disagree, because you seem to be about to cry."

She shook her head and tried to find the words to express the whirlwind that had swept through her mind. "I know that I have to move on. I know I have to keep going, but there has been something holding me back, something that I couldn't figure out that made me feel so...vacant inside. That's it. That's what I can't let go of." She sighed. She couldn't believe how simple the answer was. "I miss having that connection to someone. That's why I can't let go of Tobias. That bond ran so deep."

"You were lucky to have that," Simon gently said.

"Twice," she acknowledged. "I was lucky to have that *twice*." Carol sat back and stared at the man across from her.

Something heavy settled around them as the silence dragged on. Not awkward or uncomfortable, just *intense*. Everything that had ever passed between them had been intense. Now, however, she was smart enough to realize the ripple effects of the choices she made. She'd told Lara earlier that the last thing she wanted was to hurt Simon, and she'd meant that. Years had passed before she was able to see beyond the grief of losing Katie and the shame of cheating on John to fully understand how much she must have hurt Simon.

Simon had loved her so much that he'd taken steps toward the future they'd dreamed up together. And she'd left him holding an empty bag. She'd been selfish and unfair and had undoubtedly broken his heart. He'd simply been too kind to tell her so.

"Say it," Simon quietly encouraged. "Whatever you're thinking. Say it."

Carol inhaled deeply. "Leaning on you to get me to the other side of this would be incredibly easy. You'd probably let me because that's who you are. But I can't be that person again, Simon. I can't count on you to carry me through my problems. I don't want to hurt you like I did before, and I worry that if I let my guard down around you, we're going to head that way."

He shook his head. "We both made mistakes back then. We both did things we didn't think through. We're older now. Definitely wiser."

"God, I hope so," she muttered with a slight grin.

"We're smart enough to recognize that we're each having to figure out our futures on our own. But I don't think helping each other along the way would hurt. Do you?"

She considered his question for a moment. "Actually, I think that'd be nice. I think that'd be *very* nice."

He picked up his silverware and turned his attention to his dinner. "Which leads me back to this retirement business. I'm going to need your help writing a letter that makes me sound brilliant and humble."

"Brilliant *and* humble," she repeated as she also shifted her attention to her plate. "At the same time?"

"Preferably," he said. "Like sixty percent brilliant, forty percent humble."

She laughed as she cut into her steak, once again thankful that he knew how far to go before veering in a different direction.

# SEVEN

CAROL SAT on Mary's front porch with a cup of coffee cradled in one hand and her worry stone in the other. Brushing her thumb over the engraving, she wondered what Harold would tell her if he were sitting here watching the steady rain with her. She'd been restless the night before. Simon hadn't intended to point out something Carol had been missing, but he had.

Spending that time with Simon had reminded her of how they used to be, and there was a hint of what they could be again. Friends. Good friends. Friends who talked about problems with the intent of solving them, not simply complaining or venting. They had a common goal of easing the other's distress by offering logical advice and asking questions to peel back the layers and see what really lay beneath the surface.

No matter how many times they tried, two subjects had

dominated their dinner conversation: Simon's discontent with his job and Carol's grieving process.

After lingering at the table much longer than dinner and dessert took to eat, they'd shifted their visit to the sidewalk outside the restaurant. They'd stood under the bright lights for another hour, despite the damp chill in the air. They probably would have stayed longer, but Mary had called to check in on Carol. That was the prompt needed to break up her reunion with Simon.

Even then, they'd stood for several minutes before hugging each other tightly. When she'd left the restaurant, she couldn't stop herself from smiling.

Which nagged at her until it became something for her to pick apart until she couldn't sleep.

She was continuing her obsessive overanalysis when Elijah parked on the curb. She narrowed her eyes to peer through the rain, confirming he was alone in the car. Rarely did he visit Mary without his three daughters in tow. However, they were getting older, and being Grandma's girls wasn't quite as exciting as when they were younger. Even rushing up to hug Aunt Carol was losing its sparkle. After the first few times they saw her during this Thanksgiving visit, they were fairly casual about spending time with her. She didn't blame them. Adolescence wasn't meant to be spent hanging out with adults.

Even so, not seeing her nieces in the car gave Carol a sense of dread. She'd dealt with Mary's concerns and Lara's fears, but she'd yet to have to listen to what Elijah had to say about her being on the road long-term. She suspected she was about to find out.

He strolled toward the house as if the falling rain didn't bother him. He was tall like Tobias had been, but Elijah had a lean figure where Tobias had maintained the muscular physique he'd had when she'd fallen in love with him so long ago. Even with the differences in build, there was no denying they were brothers. They looked, walked, and acted the same.

"Hey, sis," Elijah said as he climbed the stairs.

"Where's your entourage?"

"They didn't want to come out in the rain." He sat next to her and wiped a hand over his head. "What are you doing out here?"

"Counting raindrops," Carol said. "There's fresh coffee."

"I had to cut back." He put his hand to his stomach. "It was tearing me up."

"You know, you can buy a brand with less acid."

He snickered. "If a cup of coffee doesn't peel the paint off a car, Lara won't drink it."

Carol grinned as her brother-in-law stretched his legs out and settled in beside her. She waited. And waited. Finally, she looked over. "What's up?"

Elijah shrugged. "Just hanging out."

"Right," she said. Nobody in this family was as innocent as they tried to pretend. She knew what was up. He was just biding his time until he found the right way to approach her dinner with Simon. "Go ahead. Ask."

"Ask what?"

The similarities between him and Tobias used to tug at her heart. Now she could appreciate how much the brothers were alike. Tobias and Elijah had been closer than any two siblings Carol had ever met. Their father had left when they were young. Though Mary's brother, Jerry, had been around to help out, Tobias had taken on the role of keeping Elijah out of trouble. He'd pushed his younger brother to aim higher than anyone could have ever expected them to reach.

"I had a good time last night," she said instead of playing games. "Catching up with Simon was nice. Because he's a friend. And having dinner with a friend is fun." She sipped her coffee, waiting for his reaction.

"I'm glad. You deserve to have a nice evening out."

She waited for more, but he silently stared out at the street. Though Carol couldn't possibly know Elijah as well as she knew Tobias, they both had the same pensive look when trying to find the right words to say.

"I'm not interested in dating him," she stated, sparing Elijah from his struggle. "So don't even suggest that."

"I wasn't going to."

"Because the thought didn't cross your mind, or because Lara warned you against it ahead of time?"

His lip curved up into a mischievous smile. "She said you ripped her a little bit."

"A little bit. She was being a little pushy."

Chuckling, Elijah continued watching the raindrops falling onto the street. "She also said you got pissed when she suggested you move in with us."

"Not pissed," Carol countered. "I'm simply not interested."

"That was my idea," he said as he glanced at Carol. "So don't be mad at her."

"I just said I wasn't pissed. But I'm not moving in with you guys." She looked out at the street when a car went by far too fast for a residential street. "Thanks for the offer, but I've got my own life. As pathetic as it may be."

He was quiet for a few moments before he said, "The last thing I told my brother was that I was going to take care of you. I don't know if he heard me or not, but I promised him. And I'm not going to let him down."

Her heart twisted in her chest at the way his voice strained. The emotional shift was subtle, but she heard his underlying pain. An image filled her mind—Elijah leaning over Tobias's bandaged body, whispering a promise in his ear moments before they turned the respirator off and let him go. Blinking rapidly, she forced the vision away.

"You're not letting him down," she told Elijah.

"I'm not trying to, but your ass ain't making this easy, Carol," he stated.

She chuckled, embracing the lighter comment he'd added. "Well, I'm sure Tobias told you more than once that I rarely do make things easy."

Elijah grinned. "He might have said something about that."

Putting her hand on his arm, she squeezed. "You *are* taking care of me, Elijah."

His smile faded as he shook his head. "No, I'm not. I can't take care of you when you're on the road."

"You have been there every time I've needed you," she reminded him. "You came to Houston when I needed you. You arranged his funeral because I couldn't. My God, you even helped me take care of my terminally ill ex-husband when we came through town. I think you've lived up to your promise."

Elijah considered her words before shaking his head. "You're struggling without Tobias here. We can all see that."

"Don't you think things were a bit more concerning when I wasn't?" She lifted a brow when he stared at her. "I spent the first year after losing him not feeling anything. That should have been far more worrisome to you guys, Elijah."

"I guess. Maybe pretending you were okay was easier when you were going about life as usual."

She frowned and turned her attention back out at the road as another car passed, sending a spray of water over Elijah's car. "I wasn't in a good place when John found me over the summer. I was in that scary robotic mode I get into when I can't handle things. I might be struggling now, but at least I'm not pretending that everything is okay. Nothing is okay." She swallowed before emotion could form a lump in her chest. "Things will never be like they were before, but I'm figuring out how to keep going. I'm doing the best I can. I actually had a really big revelation last night."

He looked at her expectantly but didn't push.

"Simon made a comment about how much he'd missed our conversations. We used to really delve into topics and pick them apart. I realized, *that's* the void. That's the emptiness I couldn't put a name on. You remember how Tobias would get."

"That man could overanalyze a menu," Elijah muttered. "That's why you were such a good fit. You do the same thing."

Carol shrugged. "That's why I've been having such a hard time figuring out what the next step should be. I've picked my life apart a dozen times, but without Tobias there to help me examine the pieces, I haven't been able to make sense of them. I have to figure it out on my own now. Until last night, I didn't realize that was why I've been unable to pinpoint the issue. Now that I have, maybe I can start putting the pieces together again."

"Maybe Simon could help."

She lifted a brow at Elijah, tempted to warn him about trying to push her toward something she wasn't ready for, but then she conceded. "Maybe. Someday. But I was very clear with him and with Lara, and now I'll make this clear to you: I'm not going to start something when I don't even know who I am right now. I'm still grieving, but I'll be okay. I don't want you to worry about me."

"I'm going to worry about you anyway."

"Well," she said and then frowned, "maybe you could try to not worry so much."

Sitting forward, he rested his elbows on his knees. "Just promise me you'll come to us if you need us. Don't act like we aren't your family anymore."

Carol's heart tightened. She hadn't considered that maybe her family had the same underlying fear that she'd had. That somehow, they wouldn't be family anymore once she let Tobias go. She wasn't going to let that happen. No matter what the future held. "You're always going to be my family, Elijah. *Always.*"

"In that case—" he gestured out at the street as a little yellow car drove by "—slug bug."

"Don't you dare!" The warning had barely left her mouth before he playfully punched her in the thigh.

Elijah jumped up and rushed toward the front door before Carol could retaliate the way that Tobias would have —with a harder blow.

"I'm telling your mom," Carol threatened.

However, as the door closed behind him, she chuckled. If Tobias had been here, they would have hit each other so hard they both would have had bruises. Then, they would have laughed about the inevitable bruising. Carol pushed herself up and carried her mug into the house, excited to hear the lecture Mary was going to give Elijah for "carrying on with such foolishness." She hadn't heard Mary give one of those speeches in a long time.

---

*Carol hated the ball of nerves that formed in her stomach as Tobias drove them toward his mother's house. She was too damn old to feel this nervous meeting her boyfriend's family. She wasn't a teenager, and she definitely wasn't the same weak little girl who needed everyone's approval. That was Caroline, and she'd left Caroline far behind her.*

"Stop thinking so hard," Tobias said. "I can hear your brain cranking away over there."

"What if your mom doesn't like me?" Carol blurted out.

"She's going to love you."

"How do you know?"

Tobias gave her the smooth smile that made her melt. "Because I love you."

She stared, unmoving, as her brain processed his words. He'd never said that to her before. They'd been together for months, but he'd never said he'd loved her. Until this moment. The words caused her heart to flip over in her chest.

He chuckled. "You're supposed to say, 'Oh, baby, I love you too. You're everything to me. I couldn't live without you because you're so handsome and perfect and have a huge—'"

"Oh my God!"

He laughed. "Heart. I was going to say I have a huge heart. What were you thinking?"

"Stop it," she said as heat settled over her cheeks. "I'm about to meet your mother. I don't need to be thinking about your big...heart."

Tobias chuckled, but his smile faded as he took her hand. Keeping his eyes on the road, he kissed her knuckles and then pulled her hand to his chest. "I was being real. I love you, Carol." This time, his declaration was sweet. Sincere.

"I love you too," she whispered. And she meant it. She was terrified by how much she meant loved him. There was so much he didn't know about her. Her broken marriage. Her daughter. She had an entire life that she hadn't shared with him. She hadn't been brave enough yet. Looking out the window as he *turned into a neighborhood with small brick houses, she tried to make the words form.*

*John. Katie.*

*Those were names she hadn't said in so long that they were foreign to her now. She thought of her little girl every day, but Carol couldn't remember the last time she'd said Katie's name out loud. Few people in her new life knew that her daughter had ever existed. Talking about the past was too difficult.*

*"There you go again," Tobias said, "thinking so hard your brain is about to malfunction."*

*She blinked several times before facing him, trying to find the words to tell him that there was an entire side of her that he didn't know about. She'd been a wife and a mother. She'd lived a life before ever meeting him.*

*Why the hell couldn't she tell him? What was she so damn scared of?*

*Tobias tightened his hold on her hand. "Hey, if you aren't ready to meet my family—"*

*"I am." She smiled. "Are you kidding me? You've told me so much about them, I feel like I know them already."*

*"Mama said the same thing. She said if I didn't bring you by soon, she was going to track you down herself." He kissed Carol's knuckles again. "But if you need more time, that's okay."*

*"I don't." Shaking her head, she forced thoughts of her past away. "I want them to like me. That's all."*

*"They will. But if they don't," he said, "that's okay, because what we have isn't about them or anyone else. What we have is good and right. That's all that matters."*

*She wished she could believe that, but she'd been married to*

MARCI BOLDEN

*a man her parents had loathed. She knew the toll that would take on them eventually. If his family didn't approve of her for whatever reason, Carol would walk away. She wouldn't put Tobias through the constant strain that had existed between her parents and her ex-husband. Bringing discontent to his family was the last thing she wanted.*

*"Does your mom know I'm older than you?"*

*Tobias chuckled like he did whenever their age difference came up. "How many times do I have to tell you that doesn't matter? Five years, Carol. You have five years on me. Mama will probably appreciate that. She'll say at least one of us is grown."*

*Carol smiled, though the idea of what beyond five years had taught her made her heart feel heavy.*

*Moments later, Tobias parked in front of a small house and grinned at Carol. Cupping the back of her head, he pulled her close and kissed her sweetly. "Mama's gonna love you as much as I do. I promise."*

*The knot in Carol's stomach didn't ease until they walked into the house. She had just shrugged out of her coat when Tobias's mother rushed into the living room, wiping her hands on a towel. Mary's eyes widened, and a smile broke across her lips. Opening her arms, she made her way toward Carol and Tobias.*

*"Mama," he said, "this is—"*

*"The woman who makes my baby so happy." Mary wrapped her arms around Carol and hugged her like they'd known each other forever. "I'm so happy to finally meet you."*

*"—Carol," Tobias finished flatly.*

*Carol's fears seemed foolish as she leaned back and smiled*

160

*down at the woman who'd embraced her. When Mary looked at Carol, there was nothing but affection in her eyes.*

*"Tobias has been talking about you for so long," Mary said, taking Carol's hand and leading her farther into the house. "I told him if he didn't bring you over soon, I was going to track you down myself."*

*Carol peeked over her shoulder at Tobias, who simply shrugged as if his point had been made. His point had been made, and she was happy to let him be right. By the time Mary sat down on the sofa, pulling Carol with her, Carol's fears had abated. She was welcomed here. She was embraced. Just like Tobias had told her she would, she immediately felt like family.*

———

Carol set flowers against the headstone as she traced the engraving of her husband's name. The last time she was at his grave, she'd sprinkled a bit of Katie's ashes to leave with Tobias. She'd told him so many times over the years how much Katie would have loved him, and she believed that. She could almost picture how Katie would have clung to him as she talked his ear off. Standing there now, Carol felt as if she was visiting both of them. She let out a long sigh as the familiar sadness pulled at her heart.

"Hey," she said as she rested her palm against the granite. She blinked away the tears gathering in her eyes. "I wish I could talk to you one more time. I need to see you *one* more time. Then maybe…" She bit her lip as her emotions swelled. "Who am I kidding? One more time wouldn't be enough."

Closing her eyes, she pictured the garden he'd grown at their house in Houston. She imagined his voice and the scents and did her best to transport herself back in time to when she used to sit at the little table and watch him baby-talk his plants. She imagined the *Salvia dorisiana* that had been his favorite. The fruit-scented sage was like a magnet for him. He'd rub the leaves, touch the vibrant buds, and tell the plants how lovely they were.

One memory more than all the others came to surface. She recalled Tobias cutting back a few leaves of a hosta to give a stray bunch of daffodils the sunlight to grow. The flowers had spread beyond the area where Tobias had planted them, but instead of digging them up and relocating them, he had decided to leave them be.

"Sometimes you have to let go of your plans and see where life takes you," he'd said, justifying leaving the flowers in the wrong place. He'd turned and smiled at Carol as he gave her a wink. He did that when he dropped some subtle bit of wisdom. "Sometimes the universe has bigger plans for us than we have for ourselves."

Carol had shaken her head and let out a dismissive chuckle as he went back to encouraging the plants to keep growing, even if they weren't thriving where he'd wanted them to.

Returning her attention to his grave, Carol stared at the markings in the smooth stone. "This was not part of some bigger plan. I refuse to believe this was supposed to happen. You weren't supposed to die." She sniffed deeply, trying to keep her feelings in check. "Neither you nor Katie were supposed to die."

The gray clouds above Carol parted enough to let a beam of light shine through. As in Arizona, Tobias was shining down on her, breaking through the clouds in her mind to show her the way out. That made her think of Harold, which made her think of the quartz she'd taken to carrying with her everywhere.

Pulling the stone from her pocket, she brushed her finger over the message.

*No Regrets.*

Those might not be the exact words Tobias would have used if they could have that one final talk she'd wished for, but that would have been his message to her. If she kept holding on, refusing to let go of the plans they'd made, she was going to wither in the shadows like those daffodils would have. She had to make her way back to into the light, or she would think back on her life with regret.

Carol scoffed quietly. Squeezing the quartz in her hand, she stared up at the beam. "Yeah. Okay. I get it. I don't like it, but I get it." She kissed her fingertips and then pressed them to his name before heading for the car she'd driven to the cemetery—the car that used to be Tobias's. Mary and Elijah had flown to Houston when Carol was packing up the house and had taken the car and several boxes back to St. Louis with them. Boxes that Carol still hadn't finished unpacking.

The drive back to Mary's went faster than usual, like time was speeding up around Carol. Or like her mind was only half-aware—which was much more likely. That was the tool she'd used to cope. The very mechanism she'd been fighting to unlearn.

She couldn't slip back into that way of life, where every blurry day was the same as the last because that was easier. She couldn't keep taking the easy way.

Instead of going inside Mary's house, Carol sat on the porch, sinking into the same chair she'd occupied earlier in the day when Elijah had shown up. She'd sat on this porch with Tobias so many times over the years, sitting in silence, talking about nothing, talking about everything... The conversation, or lack thereof, never mattered. They'd found harmony simply being in each other's company. For over twenty years, he was the calm to her storm, and now she had to find a way to soothe herself.

She'd failed miserably up to this point, but she was starting to sort out the reasons why. As Dr. Baxter had told her several times, acknowledging the problem was the first step to solving the problem. And the problem was, Carol had simply been too terrified to let Tobias go. She was too afraid to leave the safe harbor he'd always been for her.

"Where's your mind, baby?" Mary asked, coming out of the house.

Offering a weak smile and a shrug, Carol said, "The usual."

Easing into the chair next to Carol, Mary was quiet for a few beats. "Want to talk about it?"

Carol didn't. However, given her new goal of no longer bottling up her feelings, she said, "I feel like I'm trapped on a sinking ship in a hurricane. I have to jump into the raging waters, and when I do, I know I'll be able to swim to shore, but..." She smirked. "Well, you know how I feel about water."

"Jumping means leaving a part of yourself behind that's made you feel safe for so long," Mary offered. "The unknown is scary. But hanging on to your grief isn't a life."

Carol grasped Mary's hand. "He's not there to catch me now. He's always been there to catch me."

"You're not jumping alone, Carol. We're here with you. It's not the same, but we're not going to let you get lost."

After taking a few deep breaths, Carol nodded and said, "I'm going to head out tomorrow afternoon. Mom's pretty eager for me to get there. This will be the first Christmas we've spent together since Katie passed."

"And then what?"

"My friend wants me to go back to Houston. She's going through some tough times right now. I might stay there for a while and see how I feel about things in the spring. Being on the road isn't helping in the way I thought it would. I think I'd do better if I had a schedule. I've had a difficult time sticking to a routine living in an RV." She scoffed. "If you *ever* tell my mother she was right about that, I'll never forgive you."

Mary crossed her heart as she laughed. "She won't hear that from me." Patting Carol's hand, she said, "I wish you wanted to stay here, but you come back and see me as much as you can."

Leaning over, Carol kissed Mary's cheek, thankful for the support her mother-in-law had given her for so long. "You know I will."

# EIGHT

CAROL COULD HAVE MADE the drive between St. Louis and her mother's home outside Orlando in one day, but she'd decided to break the journey into two. She stopped at an RV park north of Atlanta and planned to stay for two days—one to decompress from the time with Tobias's family and one to prepare to stay with her mother. She loved them all, but she wanted a little quiet time to clear her head in between.

She sat at the table with a plate of leftovers Mary had packed into the RV before Carol left. Turning her laptop to face her, she glanced at the screen and smirked at the slight pout on Simon's lips. Their call this evening was a video chat, mostly because he got a new laptop and wanted to try out the webcam. He'd been rambling about his new computer while she'd reheated her leftovers.

"Bring those closer to the camera," he instructed.

"My mother-in-law spoils me," Carol informed him as

she held the plate for him to see. "Mary makes the best ribs. Literally, she's won awards. Several of them."

"I want a mother-in-law like that."

Carol returned the plate to the tabletop and picked up a barbecue-slathered rib. "There's no way I can eat this without making a mess, so when I get sauce on my face and lick my fingers, you keep your comments to yourself."

"I make no promises," he said lightly.

"Did you turn in your letter of resignation?" she asked before sinking her teeth into an incredibly tender chunk of pork.

Simon sank back on his couch and frowned. "Not yet. I know." He lifted his hands. "We spent hours writing and rewriting, but I don't feel like it's ready." Hours was an exaggeration, but they'd exchanged multiple e-mails and had several phone calls before settling on a final version.

"The resignation letter is ready," Carol countered after swallowing. "*You're* not ready."

"I am."

She shook her head. "If you were, you would have written the letter and turned it in without my input. You're smart enough to write your own letter of retirement."

"Your input was valuable."

She chewed and swallowed another bite. "But not needed. You're not ready to retire, and that's okay. Nobody is forcing you to. This is your choice, Simon. Hang on to the letter, and add your signature and the date when you're ready."

"I'm ready," he insisted. "I *am*, but I also have no idea what to do once I leave."

Carol creased her brow. "What are you talking about? Just last week, you told me how you couldn't wait to get to your property in Missouri. All the hiking, the wildlife, the quiet... Remember?"

"I remember," he mumbled. "I'm too young to retire."

She laughed at his excuse. "I retired at fifty-one. How old are you?"

He frowned. "Older than that."

"You love your job," she pointed out. "There are burdens and challenges, but you love the work. It's okay if you aren't ready to give that up."

Simon was quiet for a few seconds before raking his hand through his hair. "The thing is..."

She waited, but he didn't continue. "What?"

"I do love the job, but I think someone else could do this better." He looked at her through the laptop screen like he'd shared some great secret he wasn't supposed to utter.

She didn't respond. She needed more information before she could counter his ridiculous notion. Though they hadn't worked together for over twenty years, she didn't doubt for a moment that Simon was a perfect fit for the position. He was brilliant, considerate, and kind.

Finally, he continued. "I haven't accomplished half of what I set out to do when I accepted this position. I keep hitting roadblocks on the budget. The staff complaints are nonstop. The bickering on the board gets in the way of just about everything. Someone else could be more successful. At this point, I have to question if my ego is standing in the way of what's best for the hospital."

Carol weighed his words before announcing, "That's classic impostor syndrome."

"No—"

"Yes, it is," she insisted.

He laughed. "Look, you've been in therapy for like five minutes. You can't start tossing out diagnoses yet. You don't have nearly enough experience overanalyzing psychoses."

"*Please.* I've been overanalyzing everything since I was six." She wiped her hands on a napkin and tossed the paper aside. "Also, you don't have to be a psychotherapist to understand the basic idea of feeling too insecure for the role you're in. You have a demanding job, Simon. One that is never going to be easy for *anyone*. That doesn't make you a failure."

"I didn't say I was a failure," he clarified.

Carol grinned. "Okay, that doesn't mean someone else can do your job better. That means you're feeling overwhelmed, which is normal. Maybe you need a vacation instead of retirement."

"I got home from St. Louis last week."

"That wasn't a vacation," she reminded him. "That was four days of cramming in family time and overeating. Have you considered that maybe an extended break—an *actual* vacation—would clear your head and make some of these problems seem less insurmountable?"

He pressed his lips together for a few seconds. "I wouldn't mind hiking around the property a few times before winter sets in. That area is beautiful this time of year. I could probably put in for some time off and fly down next week." He eyed her, and she knew he was going to ask before he even said, "Would you come see me?"

"I'm halfway to Florida."

"Not today," he said. "After I get there. After Christmas."

Carol shook her head. "No. I'm staying with my mom through the holidays, and then I'm planning to head back to Houston. I miss the city and my friends. One of them is having some marital problems and could use the support. I told her I'd come after the holidays."

She saw a flash of disappointment in his eyes before he nodded.

"You could still come see me in Missouri," he told her. "Unless your friend is expecting you by a certain time. I can take vacation later. That would probably be easier anyway. We could—"

"Simon." The nerves in her stomach tensed and the warmth of a nervous blush bloomed in her chest. The rest of her thoughts jumbled into a tangled web she couldn't even begin to figure out. She needed to say more, but damned if she could find the right words.

"I'm not asking for—" he started, but she cut him off again.

"I know you're not." She sat back. "But let's be honest. If we're tucked away in the woods, just the two of us, having a good time... Things happen in situations like that, and I'm not..." Heat filled her cheeks. No doubt she was turning a similar shade to Mary's barbecue sauce. "I'm not ready for that."

"So, we don't let that happen. We're adults, Caroline."

"Yeah," she said pointedly. "We were adults last time too."

He didn't argue. He couldn't. They'd both been perfectly aware that she was married, that having an affair was irresponsible, and they'd done so anyway. Carol had put an end to things before they got too out of hand, but ending the affair didn't take away from the fact that she'd knowingly, and quite willingly, betrayed her marriage vows to John.

Carol gnawed at her lip as she tried to find the right words. "I would feel like I was committing adultery again. Not to justify what I did, but John was an irresponsible drunk. He made me miserable day after day. Tobias was nothing like that. He was wonderful. He was amazing, and in my heart, I'm still his wife. I would hate myself if I felt like I'd cheated on him. And then I think I'd turn that around until I hated you. I'm not doing that to you or to me or to my husband's memory. So... *No*. As nice as meeting you in Missouri sounds, and as tempting as spending that time with you is, I can't. Because right now, I am incredibly sad and lonely, and I don't trust myself to make the right choices."

He nodded. "Okay. I understand. I won't ask again. However, the invitation is open-ended. I had a good time at dinner last week. I'd like more of that. When you're ready."

She knew he would never pressure her to do something, but she was suddenly embarrassed about her need to explain herself. "Me too. When I'm ready."

"It's important to me that you know I'm here for you,"

Simon said. "I'm willing to help you with whatever you need."

"I understand where you're coming from, but I have to figure this one out on my own. Like you have to figure out why you're having such a hard time retiring."

She swallowed, waiting, hoping he'd follow her lead and move on from the uncomfortable topic of what may or may not transpire between them sometime in the future.

"It's the word," he said. "I'm rejecting the word. *Retirement* makes me feel old."

Her smile returned as she teased, "You *are* old."

———

*Caroline stood outside apartment number 336. Simon's apartment. He'd given her the address a few hours prior, after they'd shared a passionate kiss and agreed they could no longer deny the attraction between them. Staring at the number, she wondered what the hell she was doing. She was married—not that her relationship with John had ever been a marriage. He'd spent their wedding night drinking in a pub with his friends. Things had gone downhill from there.*

*The only reason she'd stayed was because she didn't have the heart to tear her daughter's world apart. Katie loved John, and when he could stay sober long enough, he was a wonderful father. That was the problem, though. He didn't seem to ever be sober these days. His drinking was out of control. So was Caroline's life.*

*The only thing that made sense to her these days was the way Simon Miller made her feel.*

*Calm. Centered. Worthy.*

*She'd felt the pull between them the day he'd started working at the children's hospital where she was a pediatric nurse. If she believed in something like love at first sight, she'd have thought that's what she was feeling. Then again, she had probably watched one too many of those ridiculous romantic comedies.*

*Even so, she was married. She had no business standing outside this man's apartment, knowing full well what would happen if she walked inside. Adultery wasn't something Caroline had ever considered, no matter how far apart she and John had grown. But she also hadn't considered that John was going to break her down every chance he got.*

*She couldn't think of a time when she'd been this low. Before Simon had swooped in earlier, she'd hidden in a hospital room crying after another threat of being fired for tardiness. She wasn't only upset over the fight with her boss but the fights she had to have every day. Fights with Katie to get dressed, fights with John to do anything, fights with her parents about her life choices, fights with herself about how stupid she'd been to get into this disaster of a marriage in the first place.*

*But then there was Simon, with his kind eyes and disposition. Everything about him spoke to her, to the woman she'd planned to be before she'd met John Bowman and her life had so quickly spiraled into something she couldn't recognize.*

*Was that enough to justify cheating on her husband? Even if he was a lousy drunk?*

*"The suspense is killing me."*

*Jolting, Caroline turned and noticed Simon standing several feet down the hall with a drink carrier and a bag from the doughnut shop on the corner.*

*"Are you going to knock or not?" he asked with a hint of a grin on his lips.*

*The heat of embarrassment warmed her cheeks. She put her hand to her chest to cover the telltale signs of her stress. Whenever she got embarrassed, her chest turned bright red and the bloom would spread up her neck until it enveloped her entire face.*

*Simon tilted his head. "You know I have no expectations of you, right?"*

*"I know," she said barely above a whisper. "I...I want to be here, but...I'm married, Simon."*

*Several seconds stretched by before he nodded. "How about if we have breakfast and talk about our shifts? Preferably in the comfort of my apartment. Then, you go home, and we'll see each other at work tonight."*

*She realized she must have looked ridiculous standing outside his door, staring at the number. "Okay."*

*She gave him ample room to open his front door before following him inside. As soon as she did, an odd sense of belonging washed over her. She fit here, in his clean, modestly decorated apartment, better than she ever had in the rundown ranch starter home that John had been promising to fix up for the last six years. Beyond the paint and deep cleaning Caroline had done when they'd moved in, not a repair had been made. Well, other than the basic upkeep her father-in-law had done to keep the house livable.*

Simon's apartment was crisp and neat, like the home where Caroline had always pictured herself living. Before meeting John, she'd been a premed student intent on becoming a pediatrician. She'd thought she'd have one of these apartments a few blocks from the medical district like so many of the doctors she worked with at the children's hospital. The rent was high, but the apartments were worth the price.

Walking straight to the balcony, she stared across the street. She couldn't see into the windows of the building, but being in the urban setting had a sophisticated feel that she hadn't even realized she was missing in her life. Having a young daughter meant scattered toys, splattered food, and wondering what, when, or how something got into her purse. Being the wife to a drunk only added another layer to the mysteries. Finding the can opener in the back of the freezer was the latest in the "why the hell did you do that" game she played with her husband, whose blackouts and unpredictable behaviors were increasing by the day.

"I used to picture myself in a place like this," she said, peering out the window.

Simon appeared beside her. "What changed?"

Straightening her back, she tried to push down the disappointment her life had brought her, but she didn't have the strength to pretend anymore. "I met an incredibly charming man."

"Your husband."

Caroline nodded. "Same sad story so many people have. The entire thing is boring, really."

"I'd still like to hear it."

*Facing him, not caring that he would be able to see her on the verge of crying yet again, she shrugged. "Good girl with a bright future meets bad boy who convinces her he won't ruin her life."*

*Simon shook his head. "You're far too young to consider your life ruined, Caroline."*

*For a moment, hope sparked in her heart, but she no longer had the energy to think she could find her way out of this mess she'd gotten into. She couldn't find a way out when all her strength was spent on surviving.*

*A tear slid down her cheek, and he wiped the drop away with his thumb.*

*"What has he done to you?" he asked.*

*"Nothing that I haven't allowed," she answered back. "I was young and stupid. Then, I was pregnant and scared. Now, I'm... trapped and alone. I used to tell myself I'd go back to school someday. That I could still become a doctor."*

*"You can."*

*"Katie starts school full-time in the fall. I've thought about going back then, but...he sabotages everything. He makes everything a thousand times more difficult than it should be. I don't think I can handle school right now. Maybe in a few years when Katie is older, but not now. She needs too much attention, and I can't count on him to help me."*

*Taking her hand, Simon pulled her to the couch. Sometime while she'd been staring out his window, thinking of the life she'd never had, he'd set out the food he'd brought for them. Two bagels and decaf coffees. She knew they were decaf, because even though the sun was rising, bringing a new day, they both would have to sleep soon. Working the third shift meant sleeping all day, missing out on the sunshine. Having caffeine now would keep them awake.*

*She stared at the food, watching him spread cream cheese over the bagels. "You must think I'm an idiot."*

*"No, I don't. Relationships are complex. They are filled with good, bad, and whole lot of in-between. There must be something good about your husband, or you wouldn't have fallen for him in the first place. Right?" He stared at her, pinning her down with his soft, brown eyes.*

*"Yeah. He, um, he's funny and caring. He used to make me feel like I didn't have to take life so seriously. Six years later, and I'm the only one who seems to be able to act like an adult. If I left bills and groceries up to him, we'd be homeless and starving. I feel like his mother. Everything about him is exhausting."*

*"Rumor has it he drinks a lot."*

*"Rumor has it..." She scoffed as Simon held out half a bagel to her. "That hospital is like a middle school."*

*"Most workplaces are. Does he drink too much?"*

*Caroline accepted the food and stared at the spread of cream cheese. "He always has. Things have gotten worse in the last year or so. He's rarely sober anymore."*

*"Does he hurt you when he's drinking?"*

*She lifted her eyes to his before shaking her head. "No. He's not a mean drunk. He's an irresponsible drunk. I have to hide money so I can pay the mortgage and tell him family events are two hours earlier so he might show up on time. The reason I'm late to work so often is because I have to sober him up enough to take care of Katie before I can leave the house. And before you ask, yes, I have asked him to get help. That's not a fight worth having anymore." Sinking back on his sofa, she frowned. "I don't want to talk about John."*

*"I think we should." He hesitated before facing her. "You're crying out for help, Caroline. Maybe not verbally or even intentionally, but I hear you. A lot of people hear you. We don't know how to help. You may feel alone in this, but you're not. Whatever is going on, I'm here. I want you to lean on me."*

*She didn't doubt his sincerity. That was the very trait that had brought her here in the first place. Simon was honest. Real. Caring. If she leaned on him, he would be there. He would be sturdy and strong and reliable. She missed having something real in her life. She missed having sincerity in her life. She missed having someone she could rely on.*

*In that moment, her doubts about why she'd come to his apartment faded. Her reasons for leaving were forgotten. She remembered why she was here. She was here because she needed this man to remind her that somewhere, deep inside, she was still alive.*

*Tossing the bagel onto the table, she reached for Simon and pulled him to her. Falling back onto the couch cushions, she looked up at him, hovering so close his breath warmed her face.*

*He tenderly stroked her cheek. "You don't have to do this."*

*"I want to," she said before pressing her mouth to his.*

---

Carol hadn't slept well after her call with Simon. Memories of their affair had swirled through her mind. She'd bounced between feeling guilty for mistakes of the past and guilty for thinking about Simon in a way that she was certain she shouldn't.

She'd intended to talk to Dr. Baxter about the remorse overshadowing her as well as Simon's invitation to join him in Missouri. However, her counseling session had somehow turned upside down. Rather than sorting out why she was so scared to spend alone time with Simon, Carol stared blankly at her laptop screen as Dr. Baxter talked about...*something*.

Carol nodded, and her therapist pressed her lips together in a way that Carol read as disapproval. Her father might have died years ago, but Carol remained highly attuned to that kind of subtle body language. She immediately attempted to correct her actions.

"I understand," Carol responded with a smile to counter her ill-received nod.

"Carol," Dr. Baxter said with a gentle voice, "you've said in our talks that things have been difficult with your mother in the past, but you've also indicated things have been better lately."

"Yes, they have."

"Would staying with her while we continue to delve into some of your symptoms help? Being alone may be a bit more difficult."

Another forced smile curved Carol's lips without any effort on her part. "I'll consider that."

Again, her therapist clearly saw through her. Dr. Baxter didn't have to say she wasn't buying the calm reassurances from her client. Carol could read her therapist as easily as Dr. Baxter seemed to be able to read her.

Sinking back in the bench seat at her little table, Carol let her lips fall. "I was placating again. Sorry."

Her doctor nodded. "Yes, but you recognized it. That's a good thing."

Acknowledging her inability to simply say what she was thinking had never been the problem. She knew full well that she tended to keep her thoughts to herself if she feared they'd upset someone else. "What's wrong with me?" Carol asked after a long exhale. "Why do I keep falling back on hiding behind a mask?"

"You've had a life filled with traumatic events that led to you using coping mechanisms that are no longer serving you well. Breaking that cycle is not easy, Carol."

"You're avoiding the real question," Carol stated. "What's wrong with me? Why do I do that?"

"I think you already know that you have some post-traumatic stress."

Carol shrank inside. She knew. Of course *she* knew. Having someone else know made her feel...ashamed. That wasn't a logical response. She hadn't chosen her father. She hadn't asked to lose her daughter or her husband. These were things that had been out of her control. That didn't make them any less impactful.

"You're going to add 'disorder' to make it official," Carol said flatly.

Dr. Baxter nodded. "We can make this official. You have post-traumatic stress disorder."

A knot formed in Carol's chest. "I think that's a given, considering the circumstances of Katie's death."

"Yes. But this started before Katie's death, Carol. Your tendency to disconnect emotionally began as a defense against your father's bullying. This is something you learned could protect you and is something you continue to use, even when you don't need it. The mask, as you called it, is your shield when you feel threatened, even by something as nonthreatening as the suggestion that you lean on your mother for emotional support. This is a symptom of PTSD."

Carol scoffed. "Leaning on my mother for emotional support isn't something I think I could ever feel completely comfortable with. I love her and we've made progress, but... she's still my mother."

Carol listened as the therapist explained what PTSD was and reminded Carol about the importance of having someone she could rely on, someone she trusted. This wasn't ground they hadn't covered before, but this time felt different. They were no longer talking about some distant event. Dr. Baxter had handed Carol a diagnosis. Something tangible. Something to be researched and evaluated and treated.

Carol had to admit she had a real problem now instead of simply dismissing her robotic tendencies as a quirk.

"Will you e-mail me in a few days?" Dr. Baxter asked, breaking into Carol's internal loop.

"Yes." Carol put her smile on again. "I'll be in touch soon. Thank you, Dr. Baxter." She ended the video chat and sat back.

Funny how Carol had known what was wrong for a long time, even without a professional saying the words. However, hearing Dr. Baxter confirm her suspicions made her a bit queasy. She opened a search engine on her web browser but hesitated before typing in the words.

The more she read about post-traumatic stress disorder, the harder her heart pounded. Of course, she knew the basics, the symptoms most people hear about, but the deeper she dug, the more complex the disorder seemed. The scariest part for Carol was that she could check almost every box as she read through the symptoms. Suddenly the reality that there was something wrong with her crashed down and she found thinking difficult.

She was tempted to call Simon. It was the middle of his workday, but Carol knew he'd answer. He'd stop whatever he was doing and talk her through this panic threatening to consume her. She knew he would. And she wanted him to. Which added to the stress she was already feeling. She had told him more than once that he couldn't save her. Reaching out to him now would be sending him the kind of mixed signals that she was determined to avoid. Leaning on Simon was easy, but that wasn't the answer.

She could call Mary or Lara or Alyssa. Each one would happily listen to her. So would her mother. But Carol couldn't bring herself to talk to them about this. She wasn't ready for them to jump in and try to fix this for her, because they would. She loved them for that, but as she'd told Simon, she had to save herself this time. No one could rescue her. Not from this.

Damn it. Why hadn't she faced this when Tobias was alive? Why hadn't she gotten the help he kept telling her she needed? Then she wouldn't be dealing with this alone. She'd have him. She wouldn't be having this debate. She would have called him. He would have come running. He would have wrapped her in his arms and kissed her head and told her everything was going to be okay. She would have believed him.

But he couldn't help her now. She'd waited too long.

She *always* waited too damn long.

Now she sat alone, processing what Dr. Baxter had said. Carol had been dreading facing this reality for so long. This thing that haunted her wasn't simply grief. This wasn't her working through old pain. There was something wrong with her. There was something broken inside her mind. There was a reason she was so effective at shutting down and going through life without feeling anything.

This was a method of self-defense she'd learned as a child to protect herself from her parents, who were far too hard on her, a skill she'd perfected after Katie had died. For some reason, she had convinced herself the biggest thing she had to overcome was feeling sad for her losses and finding a way to start living again. This was bigger.

She read the name again. *Post-traumatic stress disorder*.

Eyeing her phone, she again debated who to call.

No one. There was no one to call. Not for this. She had to get through this on her own.

# NINE

FLORIDA IN DECEMBER was definitely better than the winters Carol had spent growing up in Dayton. Wearing jeans and a T-shirt, she walked between her mom and aunt as they strolled through the picturesque retirement community with meticulously kept lawns and cookie-cutter one-story homes. Walking with her mom and aunt like this was almost enough to make Carol believe she could stay here for the time needed for Dr. Baxter to help sort out the mess that had become Carol's mind.

Then again...that was a hell of a mess, and Carol wasn't expecting miracles, nor could she picture herself staying in Florida for longer than a few weeks. She and her mom hadn't made *that* much progress.

"You keep getting lost," Aunt Ellen said, drawing Carol from the endless deliberation in her mind.

Carol smirked. "I was enjoying the quiet."

"Oh." Aunt Ellen grinned as she slipped her arm around Carol's and gave her niece a gentle tug. "I'll shut up, then."

Carol chuckled, but Judith wasn't amused.

"You've been unusually quiet since getting here yesterday," Carol's mom said. "What's wrong?"

There was an opening, a door swung wide, waiting for her to walk through. She could blurt out what was bothering her. She could tell her mom and aunt she had officially been diagnosed with a mental disorder. The words refused to come. She hadn't finished processing the diagnosis. Having to explain it to her mom wasn't something she was ready to deal with yet. Instead of taking the opportunity, Carol shrugged. "Why do you assume something's wrong, Mom?"

When Judith simply cocked a brow at her daughter, Carol glanced at her aunt, who stared back. Carol wasn't going to get any support from the other woman either.

Carol tried again, but she couldn't make herself share Dr. Baxter's diagnosis. "I've been trying to decide where I go from here," she said, which wasn't exactly a lie. "I thought when I was ready to settle down that I'd go back to St. Louis to be near my nieces. St. Louis has been a home to me for so long, but after being there for Thanksgiving..." She glanced around the prefect street of the retirement community. "The girls are older now, not quite as keen on hanging out with me as they used to be. I'm beginning to think that maybe I don't I belong there anymore. But if I don't belong there, then I don't know where I belong."

"Oh, honey." Ellen patted Carol's hand. "This is normal, you know. You're widowed. You don't feel like the old places in your life fit you any longer because you're not the same person you were when you had Tobias. I went through this. So did your mom." She lifted her hand and gestured grandly. "How the hell do you think we ended up here?"

Judith added, "We were two widows with no place to go. Why not Florida with the rest of the widows?"

Ellen nodded her agreement. "You've come to the point in your emotional recovery when you're going to start thinking about what comes next. You have to let go of the past and accept that finding a new life is okay. That's not easy."

"You could come here," Judith suggested. "We'd love to have you. We have room."

"Thanks," Carol said, and then she grinned. "I don't want to cramp your style."

Discounting the lame joke, Judith frowned at Carol. "I would worry less if you were here."

"We're in a good place now, Mom. Let's not risk ruining that."

Ellen piped up. "I hate that you're spending so much time alone. So much solitude isn't healthy."

"I'm not alone," Carol said. "Not really. I talk to you two almost every day. I talk to Mary several times a week. Lara and my friends are constantly texting. I'm physically alone, but I've got people to talk to all the time. I'm not alone."

"That's good, sweetheart," Ellen said. "You can't hold on to missing Tobias forever. You'll never stop feeling this emptiness if you do."

"He wouldn't want that for you," Judith said.

"No, he wouldn't." Carol swallowed hard as emotion made her throat tight. "I loved him so much."

"That will never change," Ellen said. "But he's gone. And you aren't. You gotta keep going."

"I'm trying," Carol said. "I feel like I fumble every time I even think about trying."

"There's no right way to mourn," Ellen offered.

"There seem to be a lot of wrong ways, though," Carol said. Once again, she took in the scenery as she debated her words. "Remember when I told you that I tried to go rafting?"

Ellen scowled. "Yes. That was foolish."

"I don't think my intentions were wrong," Carol said. "I think the approach was."

"You have a legitimate fear, Carol," Judith insisted.

"I had a legitimate fear twenty years ago, Mom." Stopping, she faced her mother. "Now I'm hiding from something that reminds me of things I'd rather forget. I'm *hiding*. I can't do that forever. Tobias always tried to convince me that I'm stronger than I give myself credit for. I wanted to prove to him, and to myself, that he wasn't wrong for believing that."

Ellen gently grabbed Carol's arm. "He wasn't wrong. You are incredibly strong. You've survived *so* much."

"I want to try again. Will you guys help me?" Carol asked.

Judith's jaw dropped. "Help you..."

"Get in the water," she said, determined to face her fear.

"Oh, Carol," Judith muttered. "That's not a good idea."

"Please," Carol begged. "I couldn't do it alone, but maybe

if you were there to help me, getting into the water wouldn't feel so traumatic."

Ellen dropped her hand and sighed. "I agree with your mother. This could actually cause you to have a major setback. You know that, don't you?"

"*Major* is probably an overstatement," Carol said lightly. If she could overcome her fear of water, she could push through anything and maybe finally set herself onto the road to recovery.

"I don't think so," Judith countered. "What does your therapist say?'

"I haven't told her I want to do this."

"Well, maybe you should," Judith snapped. "My God, talking you out of stupid shit is her job."

Carol gasped, but then she giggled. "Don't cuss, Mom. That's *Aunt Ellen's* job."

Judith scowled. "I'll cuss as much as I want when I think you're making a mistake."

Carol gave her aunt the best rendition of puppy dog eyes she could muster. "Tobias was there to push me when I couldn't take the next step. You know how I am, Aunt Ellen. He's not here now. Please. All I'm asking for is a little encouragement when I freeze."

A Judith-worthy sigh left Ellen as she shook her head. "You put yourself in the worst fixes."

Carol couldn't deny that, but this time, she was certain this was a fix she *had* to put herself into. She had to push beyond the anxiety that had plagued her for decades. Harold had stepped in before she could do that in Arizona—which wasn't necessarily a bad thing—but she needed to confront this trauma. "Is that a yes?"

"No," Judith stated. She widened her eyes at Ellen. "*No.*"

"If we don't help her, she's just going to go by herself," Ellen said.

Carol smiled at her mom. "She's not wrong. At some point, I'll do something really stupid, like climb into an inflatable raft and go over some rapids. Someone stopped me once. There's no guarantee that will happen again."

Judith pressed her mouth into a flat line and narrowed her eyes before finally spitting out, "Fine. We'll help you."

Carol kissed her mom's cheek. "Thank you."

Judith put her arm through Carol's and tugged until they started walking again. "You can thank me when you have a breakdown and we have you committed."

Carol laughed. "Well, at least I wouldn't have to figure out where to settle down." Pulling her mom to a stop, Carol let her smile fade as she looked into blue eyes that mirrored her own. "I have to do this, Mom. I want to move on with my life, but there are things that won't let me. I have to face them."

Judith put her hand to Carol's face. "I know, but I don't think this is the way."

"Well, running hasn't worked. This can't be any worse. Can it?"

———

*Carol hated Christmas. She'd managed to avoid celebrating it ever since Katie had died. Last year, the first Christmas she and*

*Tobias should have spent together, she'd told him how sorry she was that she had to work. This year, however, she was working at a company that was closed on Christmas. She and Tobias were sharing an apartment. His family was having a big get-together.*

*She couldn't avoid Christmas this year. That realization was slowly killing her.*

*She wanted to embrace the new life she'd found. Tobias was incredible, his family was everything she'd never had before, but as they walked through the Christmas tree farm, her heart was hollow. Hearing the music that Katie use to sing and seeing kids darting around laughing made her want to curl up in a ball and disappear.*

*Tobias put his arm around her shoulder and hugged her close. "How are you doing?"*

*Several answers danced through her mind. They were all lies. She wasn't okay. She wasn't fine. She was devastated. "Not good," she answered honestly because he'd see through anything else.*

*Stepping in front of her, he leaned in until she tilted her face up at him. "Do you want to leave?"*

*"You wanted a live tree," she pointed out.*

*"I don't have to have one. Or I can come alone. You can wait in the car."*

*She closed her eyes when three kids ran by them, excitedly yelling over one another about the tree they wanted. "She loved Christmas," Carol whispered.*

*"I bet she did," Tobias said gently. "I bet she tore into her*

*presents so fast she never even knew what she got until there wasn't a wrapped box under the tree."*

*A knot formed in Carol's chest as memories flashed through her mind. She bit her lip so she didn't cry in the middle of the walkway. She was mildly successful until Tobias pulled her close and embraced her in his big arms. She buried her face in his chest as he held her. He kissed her head several times before releasing her.*

*"I bet Katie would want the biggest tree here, wouldn't she?" he asked.*

*Carol laughed dryly. "Actually, she'd probably want the ugliest tree. She'd want to rescue it and make it pretty. She favored the underdog."*

*Tobias pointed to the discounted section of trees that had broken limbs, lopsided trunks, and missing bristles. "Let's rescue us a tree."*

*"No, Tobias," she said with a shake of her head. Carol knew he wanted a big tree with lush limbs to hang the ornaments they'd bought. As they'd selected the red and white decorations, he'd excitedly talked about how they were going to get the best tree on the lot. She tried to steer him toward the better-looking options, but he was stronger. With one firm tug, he yanked her to his side and headed for the ugly trees. "You don't have to do this."*

*He winked down at her, and the tenderness in his eyes nearly melted her. "Yeah, baby, I do. You said Katie would want an ugly tree. I'm getting her an ugly tree." He grinned. "I'm getting her the ugliest damn tree I can find." Brushing Carol's hair back, his smile faded. "Is this the first Christmas you've celebrated since losing her?"*

*Carol didn't respond. She didn't have to. He obviously knew before he'd even asked.*

*"Being sad is okay, Carol. Hurting is okay. I'm here for that. I'm right here to help you through. Okay?"*

*"I love you," she said, but the words barely came out.*

*"I love you." He hugged her again. This time, when he turned toward the ugly trees, she didn't try to stop him.*

*Within an hour, she stood holding a scrawny blue spruce with mostly naked limbs while Tobias screwed the trunk to the base. Stepping back when the tree was secure, she shook her head at the sickly thing.*

*"I can't believe this is our first tree," she grumbled.*

*Tobias smiled up at her from the floor. "It's great. It's perfect."*

*"It's a mess."*

*Pushing himself to his feet, he stepped beside her to admire the evergreen. After a moment, he chuckled, and then the laugh ripped free and he threw his head back. Carol had no choice but to laugh with him.*

*"Mama's going to offer to buy us a real tree. Just wait," Tobias said. "She's going to take pity on us."*

*Carol's smile dipped as a flash of her parents crossed her mind, but she pushed them away. They'd caused her all the pain she was going to allow. Besides, she had enough misery on her mind thinking how much she missed Katie. She wasn't going to let her parents take her down even further.*

*"I saw that," Tobias commented.*

*She gazed up at him, lifting a quizzical brow.*

"This isn't the same as having Katie here," he said, apparently misinterpreting where her mind had gone, "but we're going to do everything we can to make this a Christmas she would have loved, okay?"

Warmth filled Carol's heart. "She would have loved you."

Tobias stood a bit taller. "Yeah?"

Carol nodded. "I would have told her no way we were buying this lousy tree, but here this thing is because you would have caved and spoiled her."

"Damn straight," he said, beaming. "I would have bribed that kid every chance I got."

She smiled, but then she paused. "Do you think..."

"What?"

"We should..." Carol swallowed hard and blinked as her stupid tears welled up again. "Since we can't buy her presents, can we find a shelter to donate to? She'd like that. She'd want the kids there to have presents too."

He nodded. "I'll tell Mama and Uncle Jerry. I bet they'll want to help."

"Thank you," Carol whispered. "The last two Christmases... I did everything I could to ignore them. This feels better. This is hard, but it feels better."

"You can't ignore what hurts you, babe. You have to face it." He pressed a kiss to her forehead. "I'm here now. I'll help you do that. I'll always help you do that."

Later that afternoon, Carol stood inside the community center pool house with her eyes downcast, staring at her bare feet. She and Lara had spent a morning at a salon while Carol was in St. Louis. She'd had a pedicure and chosen a bright red polish for her toenails. She didn't usually go with such vibrant colors. Looking at the shade now, she wished she'd gone with burgundy instead. She'd have to make an appointment somewhere while in Florida. Her mom wouldn't go, but maybe Aunt Ellen would be willing to join her for an hour or so of pampering.

"Are you okay?" Judith asked, distracting Carol from her rambling thoughts.

Looking at her mom, Carol blinked several times. She didn't know how much time had gone by, but her mother was being incredibly patient. That wasn't something Carol could say very often. After forcing herself to swallow, she tightened her hold on her mom's hand and refocused on the reason they were all standing there in a hot, humid, glassed-in room breathing in chemicals.

Staring at a sign on the other side of the pool that warned against diving, Carol worked up the courage and took a step closer to the pool.

Their plan, or as much of one as they'd devised, was to enter through the beach entrance. The gradual ramp, which provided pool accessibility for handicapped residents of the retirement community, was the best way to slowly enter the pool. That way, Carol could take slow, measured steps and stop her forward progress at any time.

Or so they'd decided.

Just looking at the slope where the water gently lapped at the edge made Carol's heart pound against her rib cage. Her stomach rolled, and bile rose up her throat, making her breath feel like fire every time she exhaled a short, panting burst.

"I should have had a drink first," Carol managed to say. Though she intended to make a joke, her words came out tense, breathy. Barely audible.

"I can go get the tequila," Aunt Ellen offered. Even her voice sounded tight. Ellen, who found the humor in any situation, wasn't laughing now. The tension surrounding the trio was palpable.

"Absolutely not," Judith stated.

"We have as long as you need, Carol," Aunt Ellen said. "No need to rush."

Carol lifted her gaze to the slope where they were headed, one *very* slow step at a time. "It's just water." Her voice quivered, betraying her attempted confidence. "It's just...water."

Her abdomen burned hotter. Her throat was so tight, she could hardly swallow. She forced herself to take a deep inhale through her nose, like her therapist had been telling her, and instantly regretted it. The scent of chlorine filled her nose. The harsh aroma made her knees grow weak and her already upset stomach to churn. Her body lurched as she gagged.

"Okay," Ellen soothed.

Someone ran a hand up and down Carol's back. She didn't know who was trying to soothe her, but the attempt was futile. The movement didn't have a calming effect. Carol's hyperawareness exacerbated the movement, making the touch feel like a wrecking ball rolling over her spine. She didn't have the strength to ask whoever was making the effort to stop. She was too focused on the pool.

"This is enough," Judith said. "Let's stop now."

"I'm okay," Carol insisted.

After pulling her hand free from Carol's grip, Judith flexed her fingers several times. "The hell you are."

"I'm going to have to agree with your mom, kiddo," Aunt Ellen said. "This is too much. Let's call it a day and try again tomorrow."

"I can't keep putting things off until tomorrow," Carol said. "Tomorrow might not come."

The other women were silent, and Carol suspected they were casting concerned glances at each other behind her back. Determined to prove to them and to herself that she could do this, Carol took another tentative step toward the pool.

Damn it. Why had she waited so long to try to overcome this? Why hadn't she let Tobias do this with her? He'd offered numerous times over the years. If he were there, she could look into his face, focus on his voice, and let him gently coax her along.

"I'm going to close my eyes," Carol said. "You guys...lead the way."

She disregarded their silence as she let her eyes drift shut. As her mom and aunt helped her take a step forward, Carol pictured the garden Tobias had planted. She pictured how the wide variety of flowers danced in the breeze. Blooms of every color complemented one another to create a picture-perfect scene. He loved to tend to each and every one as if they were each precious to him.

*Salvia dorisiana* had been his favorite, though. The sage had a sweet scent and bright pink flowers that drew him in like the bees that came every day to gather pollen.

She could hear Tobias's voice now. The low timbre rolled through her like a distant rumble of thunder.

"Look at you," he'd say to whichever plant had drawn his attention. "Growing like a weed." Then he'd chuckle at his own joke.

"You're not funny," Carol had told him every time he'd make the pun, which was far too often.

"They think I am," he'd say. Then he'd lean in and smell a bud. "Don't you?"

Carol gasped when water splashed against her toes. She jolted and, once again, started to pant as her lungs restricted. Panic was taking hold. Fear was overcoming her. Just like the water could overcome her...surround her, pull her in, take her under...

A memory flashed through her mind in jumbled bits.

John. Katie. Screaming. Crying.

"Slow down," Ellen said with a firm but gentle tone. "You don't want to hyperventilate."

Carol focused on her breathing. In. Out. In. Out. She was almost calm when a different voice crept into her mind.

"Mama," Katie called from somewhere in Carol's memory. "Mama, *lookit*. See what I can do?"

A sob worked up Carol's throat and echoed through the pool house.

"That's far enough," Judith said, pulling Carol's mind to the present.

Carol shook her head. "No." Forcing herself to keep going, she slid one foot forward and then the other, until water lapped at her ankles.

When she and John were sprinkling Katie's ashes in the Pacific Ocean, he'd put his hands to her face and forced her to focus on his eyes as he coaxed her forward. Never in her life did Carol think she'd pull a memory of her ex-husband to the surface to soothe her, but she did now.

She pictured his blue eyes as he'd stared into hers.

"I'm right here with you," John had said as he'd urged her deeper into the water. "You can do this."

Before she knew it, the water was splashing at her knees. With a few more tentative steps, the water was at her thighs and then her hips.

This was it. This was the deepest she'd been in the water for over twenty years. Swallowing hard, she tried to settle the elephants stampeding around her stomach. Her heart pounded against her rib cage. Fear screamed at her to stop, to turn around.

She took another step. Then another.

When the water reached her waist, she forced her eyes open. She gazed through the clear water at her feet with the bright red tips. Red like...rain boots.

Squeezing her mom's hand, Carol clung to her, hoping to stop the memories from coming back. Though she was wearing the waterproof shorts she'd bought to go rafting because she didn't own a swimsuit, she saw herself dressed in Scooby Doo scrubs. Though she was barefoot with bright red toenails, she saw an old pair of tennis shoes.

She couldn't stop the racking sobs that hit her. They hit her hard, stealing the oxygen from her lungs, breaking her heart as her trauma resurfaced.

"Enough," her mom insisted, tugging Carol's hand. "*Please*. Caroline, this is enough."

Instead of letting her mom pull her back to the edge, Carol forced air into her lungs and let her knees fold until she was fully submerged.

She hadn't been under water in decades. Hadn't felt her hair float around her face. Hadn't heard how the beating of a heartbeat was amplified underwater. The pounding echoed through her ears. Anxiety filled every bit of her until she might burst. Carol sat on the bottom, focused on her fear, making herself feel every emotion this moment was forcing on her until two sets of hands pulled her up.

She gasped for air as she broke the surface. Breathless, she met her mom's concerned gaze.

Judith frown as she wiped water from Carol's face. "That's enough," she said again. This time. her voice trembled and tears caused her eyes to shimmer. "Please. No more."

Carol fell into her mom, embracing her as she sobbed. Judith held her and hugged her close for a long time. But then, Carol's fear and sadness changed to something else. "Oh no," she muttered, pulling away. "I think I'm gonna—"

"Oh my," Judith muttered as Carol leaned over and vomited into the pool.

"Clean up on aisle two." Ellen giggled at her comment, even though no one else did.

Carol lurched again, heaved several times, and then stood up. "Oh. Sorry."

"Don't worry," Judith said as she brushed wet strands of hair from Carol's face. "This is a community of old people. You wouldn't believe the things the cleaning crew has had to scoop out of this pool."

Carol wiped her mouth with the back of her hand as she grimaced at the water where she'd been submerged. "*Ew.*"

# TEN

CAROL PULLED the blue and green tartan blanket tighter around her as her mom set a cup of tea on the end table. Tearing her attention from the twinkling white lights on the small tree they'd decorated earlier in the day before they'd gone to the pool house, Carol muttered her thanks.

Judith eased down and put her hand on Carol's knee. "How are you?"

Rather than admit her head was throbbing from her spiked blood pressure or that she was so emotionally drained she could sleep for weeks, Carol said, "I'm okay, Mom. I'm sorry about today. For some reason, I thought going into the pool would help, but..." Her words trailed off, and they sat quietly for several moments.

"Nothing is going to make losing your husband or your daughter better, Carol. You have to know this by now. All you can do is find a way to carry on."

"I'm working on that."

"I don't think—"

Carol closed her eyes. "Mom. Please don't try to tell me how to cope with all the things I've gone through. Please. I know you're worried, I appreciate that, but you can't help with this. You just can't."

Judith was quiet for a few moments before saying, "Seeing you suffer, knowing I can't help you, is the hardest thing I've ever been through. I've never felt so helpless in my life because I know nothing I do is going to help. If I could take all your pain away, I would."

Carol sniffed as she gripped her mom's hand. "But you can't."

Putting her arm around Carol, Judith gave her a slight hug and kissed her temple. "You're doing great. I don't tell you that enough, but it's true. I'm really proud of you."

"Thanks," Carol said. "I'm proud of you too. We've both overcome some really tragic things."

"*I've* overcome them," Judith clarified. "You're a work in progress."

Despite her miserable mood, Carol chuckled. However, her smile faded quickly. "I hate Christmas," she confessed. "Every year seems worse than the one before. I feel so empty during the holidays."

"Well," Judith said quietly, "this is the best Christmas I've had in a long time. This is the first one we've spent together since we lost Katie."

Tears bit at Carol's eyes, and she sniffed. "I would do so many things differently if I could."

"But you can't," Judith reminded her. "None of us can. We can only move forward."

"Oh," Carol moaned. "Did you slip a life lesson in there?"

"I tried."

Carol shook her head. "I can't get used to how...human you are now."

"It's the medication," Judith countered and then smiled. She hugged Carol closer. "I wish I'd been brave enough to get help sooner. Maybe you wouldn't have gone through so much of this on your own. But I am very happy you're getting help now."

"Me too."

"What you did today was very brave," Judith said.

Carol snickered. "Tell that to the maintenance man."

"Tobias would be proud."

"I hope so."

"He would be." Judith put her head to Carol's. "So would your dad," she whispered.

Carol pressed her cold fingers against her closed eyes. "God, I miss him so much. I never thought I would say that."

They were quiet for several seconds before Judith patted Carol's hand. "I picked out something special for you for Christmas, but I want you to have it now. I'll be right back."

After snagging a tissue from the box on the end table beside her, Carol dried her eyes and wiped her nose. She frowned at the empty wineglass beside her, debating if she wanted to get up to refill her drink or not. Her mom had brought her tea, but that wasn't going to take the edge off her raw emotions. Not unless her mom fixed tea the way Aunt Ellen did—with a hefty shot of tequila.

The odds of that were not in Carol's favor. She opted to take a sip to test the drink. Her mom hadn't even added sugar.

"*Nasty*," Carol mumbled, scrunching up her nose.

"I found this after your last visit," Judith said, walking back into the room. "I'd packed this away when I moved here and hadn't seen it since."

Carol accepted the small, Santa-covered gift bag from her mom. Taking the red tissue paper from the top, she reached in and pulled out a framed photo she'd never seen. The picture had been taken on Katie's sixth birthday, a few weeks before she'd died. Carol's dad had draped one arm around Judith and the other around Carol. Katie stood in front of them, beaming brightly in her purple birthday dress and the red rain boots she rarely took off.

Though the three adults in the image barely spoke to one another at the time, they were all smiling. Carol had no doubt John's mother had directed them how to pose for the photo. She was always trying to help make things better between Carol and her parents. Throwing Katie into the mix had clearly done the trick. There wasn't a bit of evidence of the tension that was boiling right below the surface.

Carol had never seen the photo. She'd probably left Ohio before the film had even been developed. Katie hadn't lived long after the picture had been taken, and Carol hadn't stuck around long after that. In fact, this had to have been the very last picture ever taken of the four of them together. One of the last pictures ever taken of Katie.

"This was a good day," Judith whispered.

Carol took a few breaths before shaking her head. "John and I tried so hard to give her a good life, but we fought so much. Katie knew."

Judith pointed to the picture. "Look at her smile, Carol. She had a wonderful day. She was so happy. Focus on that. She loved you. So did your dad." Judith kissed Carol's head. "So does your mom."

Carol hugged the photo to her chest as her tears welled again. "I love you too, Mom. Thank you for this. I really needed to see this."

"Are you sure you want to go back to Houston so soon?"

Carol shrugged. "Alyssa wants me to stay with her for a while."

"Well, I, for one, am very happy you won't be on the road by yourself."

Carol grinned. "Oh, Mom, I had *no* idea my traveling alone made you uncomfortable."

Judith scoffed. "Not that my concerns matter to you."

"They matter." Carol took her mom's hand and entwined their fingers. "I'm glad we can talk like this now."

"So am I. We had some tough years."

Carol smirked. That was putting their rough relationship mildly, but she wasn't going to dwell on that. "My friend Simon has a house in Missouri. He asked me to visit him there."

Judith didn't respond. She likely didn't know how.

"I told him I couldn't because..." Carol didn't finish her thought.

Finally, Judith pressed. "*Because*?"

"Because talking with him now is as comforting as it was all those years ago. I'm pretty sure I can predict what would happen if we were together for too long. Even thinking that might happen makes me feel..." She scoffed. "Is it adultery if your husband is dead? Because I feel guilty even thinking that someday I might want...you know."

Judith shifted as she averted her eyes, looking around the room. "I, um, I'm probably not the one to talk to about sex."

Carol cringed. "Ugh, I'm not talking about sex. I mean... not exactly." Carol ran her hand over her face. "*Emotionally*. I feel like I'm cheating on Tobias just thinking that maybe *someday* I'll want another man to want me."

Judith shifted, opened and closed her mouth a few times, and then sighed. "I don't know, Carol." She faced the kitchen and yelled, "*Ellen!*"

Carol's heart dropped to her stomach. "No, Mom. Don't ask Aunt Ellen. Don't."

Ellen stepped into the living room with a wineglass in one hand and a bottle in the other. "What?"

"How long did you wait to have sex after Bert died?" Judith asked.

Carol sank down in the sofa. "This is not something I want to know."

"Um, about three months."

Carol's discomfort was diminished by her shock. She gawked at her aunt. "*What*?"

"His best friend was a very handsome man," Ellen justified. "Why? *Oh!* Are we talking about Simon?" Ellen practically ran into the room and sat in one of the chairs with bright eyes and a big smile. "Tell me *everything*."

———

*Every time Caroline started to feel guilty about having an affair with Simon, John would do something so incredibly stupid that her guilt was squashed with a litany of justifications. This time, Caroline had spent the day before—her only day off this week— getting quotes on repairs for the car because John had sideswiped something. He didn't even know what... Just "something." Of course he insisted the accident wasn't his fault, and sure, he'd had a beer or two, but he'd been sober enough to drive.*

*Caroline had screamed and ranted. He was a cop, for God's sake! He knew what happened when people drank and drove. He knew the destruction he could cause them or some other family. And he'd better never, ever drive drunk with Katie in the car, so help her God.*

*Her screaming had been futile. She knew as well as he did. The fights, the threats, the never-ending cycle of her threatening to wash her hands of him only to stay were over and done by the next day. Caroline had found someone to make the repairs on the car that would fit in their measly budget.*

*"Where's your mind?"*

*With a few blinks, she banished thoughts of her husband and refocused on the man she loved. "Sorry," she said and offered Simon a sweet smile.*

*"What's going on?"*

*She shook her head, knowing how their conversation would go if she mentioned her husband. Simon was as supportive as he could be, but he hadn't been very subtle in his desire for her to leave John. He hadn't outright asked her to leave John yet, but Caroline suspected the conversation would happen soon.*

*She hoped she was wrong. She didn't want to be put in a position to choose between her happiness and Katie's, and she knew that's what the choice would come down to. Eventually, though, Simon was going to broach the topic, and Caroline was going to have to stop pretending that she could have this relationship without consequence.*

*She inhaled the morning air. Their shift had ended, and like they tended to do these days, she'd followed him to his apartment. They'd made love and then moved to sit on his balcony. The little outdoor space overlooked the busy street leading to the children's hospital where they worked. Most mornings, they'd sit and have one cup of coffee before Caroline slipped from this calm, quiet world and headed to the chaos that was her home.*

*"John?" Simon pressed.*

*"It doesn't matter."*

*"I would disagree. You've been distracted all morning."*

*She grinned at him. "Not all morning."*

*He didn't even smile. "What did he do?"*

*Caroline shook her head. "Drop it."*

*"No."*

*Startled by his persistence, she gawked at him. A million rebuttals ran through her mind, but she opted to push herself up instead of engaging.* She dumped what was left in her mug down the sink when he leaned on the island across from her. Focusing on his eyes, she caved, as she tended to do.

"He wrecked the car," she stated. "The only car we have because we can't afford to get a second one. I spent all day yesterday finding someone to do cheap repairs because cheap is all we can afford. That's all we can afford because John is completely fucking irresponsible." She stared at Simon. Waiting. "This is the part when you tell me to leave him."

"If I told you to leave him, would you?"

"It's not that easy."

"It'll be that easy when you're ready."

She narrowed her eyes at him. "What does that mean?"

"That means you'll leave him when you're ready. I hope it's soon, because I love you, but you have to make that decision for yourself, Caroline. You're a smart woman. You're a good mother. You'll know when it's time."

Her defenses fell and her shoulders sagged. "I already know," she confessed. "He's never going to change. He's never going to stop making my life hell. But then I see him with our daughter, and I know he could be better. I know could he be. He's such a good father. Katie adores him." Caroline shrugged as she looked at him. "How do I reconcile leaving when I'm the only one who's miserable?"

"You reconcile leaving by remembering you matter too. Your happiness matters too. One of these days, the scales will tip far enough for you to understand that."

Her heart ached as she walked around the counter and into

his arms. *"It's not right for me to put you through this. This is my mess, not yours."*

*He hugged her close and kissed her head. "I walked into this knowing you were married. I can't exactly hold you accountable."*

*"You could," she said, leaning her head back to look up at him. She smiled. "But you're better than that."*

*"I am pretty awesome," he said.*

*She laughed and kissed him. "You're amazing, and I'm lucky to have you." After one more kiss, she pulled away. "I need to go."*

*He followed her to the door. "If I asked you to leave him, would you?"*

*She focused on pushing her feet into her worn-out sneakers. After several long seconds, she looked at him. "I don't know. Things aren't that black and white, Simon. I love you. I do."*

*"We could have an amazing life together. I'd never stop trying to make you happy."*

*She did know that. She knew that in the depths of her soul. "Katie's happiness comes first," Caroline said. "There will never be a day when I choose my happiness over hers."*

*He looked sad but pushed a smile to his lips. "That's what makes you such a good mom." He closed the distance between them and kissed her lightly. "Go home. To Katie. I'll see you at work tonight."*

*She opened the door and glanced back. The sense of dread she'd had earlier returned. As much as she loved Simon, as much as she belonged with him, this affair was going to have to end sooner rather than later.*

*Before someone really got hurt.*

———

After ignoring two calls and several texts from Simon, Carol broke down and answered his third call. Though his attempts to reach her had been spread over the last two days, she was irritated by his persistence. No. That wasn't what was irritating her. She was irritated because she hated the imbalance she'd been feeling lately. No matter how much work she put into finding her way, she ended up unsure which way to go, which step to take next.

She had convinced herself getting into the pool would somehow jar her mind free from this roller coaster, but the ride continued. Though she knew that wasn't his intent, Simon was adding to the discord hounding her.

As she connected the call, Carol walked into the spare room, which was actually Ellen's painting studio. "Hey."

Simon was quiet for a moment, and Carol realized she'd likely sounded snippy. She hadn't intended to. The last person she could blame for her irritability was Simon.

After blowing out some of her annoyance, she tried again. "How are you?"

"I'm good," he said somewhat hesitantly. "How are *you*?"

She stacked a few pillows together so she didn't feel like the cushions were swallowing her before sitting on the couch. The bright red sofa was too soft for Carol's liking, but Judith wasn't comfortable with Carol staying at the campground alone. The last time Carol had visited, her sleeping arrangements had been the source of one of the many fights they'd had. Rather than even debate the issue this visit, Carol slept on the couch that didn't offer nearly enough support.

"Tired. And maybe a little cranky," she admitted. "The sleeping arrangements at Mom's aren't up to my high standards."

Simon laughed softly. "Well, we can't always find five-star hotels when we need them."

She smiled, and some of the tension she'd been carrying eased. "She isn't comfortable with me staying at the campground, so to cater to her fears, I sleep on an uncomfortable sofa that hurts my back rather than the exceptionally comfortable mattress in my RV."

"Oh, the sacrifices we make for our parents."

"You have no idea," Carol muttered.

"I was starting to worry," he said more seriously. "Everything okay?"

Looking around the paintings hanging on the wall, Carol's gaze fell on the one that had become her favorite. Rain poured down on a woman with her arms open and her head back, her dress flowing as she danced. The image stirred a bit of foolish jealousy in Carol's heart. Even though the image was a painting, Carol was reminded that she'd never been so carefree. Something inside her had yearned for that kind of freedom for so long, but she'd never been able to give in.

She wished she could let her guard down and simply *be*.

Ellen had that ability, but Carol had been raised by Judith. Carol had spent her entire life calculating every move she made. Her entire existence had been meticulously planned. Even now, with the so-called freedom that came with being on the road, Carol managed to work out every detail before taking the next step.

That was exhausting. She was exhausted. She wished she could take a vacation from her mind and all the games it played with her. If she could escape herself for a day or two, maybe she'd feel rested. Maybe she could find her way again.

"Caroline?" Simon pulled her mind back to the conversation. "What's going on?"

"I've had a bit of a rough day," she said honestly. "I'm probably not good company tonight, Simon. I should let you go."

"No," he stated quickly, as if he feared she'd hang up without giving him a chance to respond. "Talk to me."

Carol stared at the painting again. "I think being on the road is catching up with me. I'm exhausted."

"You didn't answer my call yesterday. Did something happen?" he asked.

A flash of the pool house hit her and took her breath away. Monsters disguised as memories clawed at her, threatening to pull her apart. Pushing herself to her feet, Carol escaped in the nick of time. She stepped closer to the painting, focused on the finer details—the breaks in the strokes that weren't quite even and the spots where the brush bristles went slightly wayward.

Aunt Ellen had been an art teacher when she was younger. She'd taught Carol so much about painting, but Carol had never been able to see beyond those minor mistakes and enjoy creating images. She obsessed about the things that were wrong, losing sight of what was right.

"Hey," Simon gently coaxed. "What happened?"

"I got in the pool," she said numbly, separating herself from the anxiety the words elicited within her.

Simon was quiet for a few seconds. "How far?"

Closing her eyes, she tried to forget the feel of the cold on her face, the way her hair brushed against her cheeks, and how her clothes clung to her as her mom and aunt pulled her back to the surface. Simply thinking about those few seconds under the water made her stomach roll again. "All the way. I went under."

"That must have been difficult."

She cringed as another memory came to her. "I vomited. In the water. They had to close the entire pool for a few hours to flush the water."

He didn't laugh, but when he spoke, she could practically see the smile on his face. "I'm sure that will give the community something to talk about for a while."

"No doubt."

"How are you feeling about that today?" he asked.

"The gossip or the breakthrough?"

"Both, I guess."

She turned away from the painting to peer out the window. The near-full moon stood out against the dark sky, demanding to be seen. Looking up at the silver orb pulled a truth she wasn't sure she wanted to share. "I think..." Her voice cracked as her emotions stirred unexpectedly. "I'm so tired of feeling like I'm broken. I've felt so broken for so long, and I'm tired. Down to my bones. I'm tired."

"You're carrying a lot of weight. You're bound to feel tired from time to time."

Carol blinked several times. She'd almost forgotten she was talking to someone other than the moon. Turning from the window, she grabbed a tissue from the box on the end table and wiped her cheeks. "I'm not going to dump this on you. I'll talk to you later."

"Caroline," he called. "You're not dumping on me. I'm talking to you because I want to. I want to help you. Don't shut me out."

She closed her eyes at his plea. She'd be angry that someone else was accusing her of shutting him out, but everyone who knew her knew that was what she did. She pulled away. She locked herself away. Even Simon, a man she'd barely reconnected with after decades, knew this about her.

Wasn't that the one thing she was working the hardest to change? Her habit of shutting people out when she was hurting the most?

"I faced a really big fear," she said. "I think that's shaken me more than I realized."

"Of course it has. Growth isn't for the faint of heart," he said. "Pushing through those boundaries is painful and scary. But you did it. You faced something that has haunted you for a really long time. Of course you're shaken, sweetheart, but you faced it. Be proud of that."

She sniffed. "I'll probably never step foot in a pool again. The thought makes my heart race and my hands tremble."

"That's okay," Simon assured her. "You don't have to. Once is enough. Once is all you need to take a step forward."

Tugging a thread that had come loose on her T-shirt, Carol debated how much she should share. She knew Simon wouldn't judge her. He was better than that. But she'd spent her entire life protecting herself from what others might think. Wrapping the string around her finger, she made a deal with herself—if the string broke free when she pulled, she'd tell him; if the thin thread stayed attached to the material, she'd change the subject.

She pulled. The string broke.

*Shit.*

After licking her lips, she blurted out, "There's more. My therapist... She says I have PTSD. That's not a surprise," she said quickly. "I've been through so much. Dad, John, Katie, Tobias."

"Having someone give what you're going through a name makes it real," he said.

Hearing him say exactly what she'd been thinking made fat tears fall down her cheeks. He understood. Of course he understood. He always had.

Carol sniffed. "Apparently my ability to turn into an emotionless android at will isn't normal. Who knew? I thought having that much control over my mind was my superpower."

Once again, Simon didn't laugh, mostly because her joke was a blatantly lame attempt to make herself feel better.

"You know," he said instead, using the same tender voice, "you've been dealt a bad hand from the start. This didn't start with John."

"No, it didn't," she agreed. "I've been like this forever. Since I was a kid. Making amends with Mom let me see Dad in a different way, but that doesn't change the way I was raised. Trying to understand his parental approach doesn't lessen the cloud of intimidation I grew up under. Sympathizing with his problems doesn't take away the fear I lived with every day as a kid."

"It doesn't," Simon agreed. "You can't change the past, but now that you have a name for the thing that's haunted you, you'll be better prepared to take on the healing process." He was using the supportive and kind voice she'd heard whenever he spoke to parents about their child's health and treatment. This was the side of him she'd fallen for all those years ago. The supporter. The healer. The caregiver.

Simon was her first experience with a man who understood that kindness wasn't weakness. He'd made her realize that was the type of man she wanted. She didn't need the angry overlord like her father or the deceitful charmer like John. She'd needed the softness she'd found first in Simon and then in Tobias.

He'd taught her that she needed and deserved a man she didn't have to protect herself from. Unfortunately, as wonderful as Tobias had been, Carol had never unlearned the need to hide part of herself away. She'd never allowed herself to show him how fractured she really was.

Even if she and Simon weren't together now, she didn't

want to hide from him. She was so very weary of hiding, of protecting herself and everyone around her from the darkness she knew lurked in her mind.

She had an illness. The reason she'd felt damaged for so long was because something *was* damaged. Something that could be treated. Something that could be healed. Despite the losses, the pain, the traumas...she could heal. Hearing Simon acknowledge, understand, and open the door to help her take the next step gave her a stirring of hope she hadn't felt in some time.

Putting her hand to her face, she forced herself to keep her tears at bay. "Okay," she said, her voice heavy from the emotions she was fighting. "I have a name. Now what?"

"Now you work with your doctor to find the best treatment. This is like any other illness, Caroline. You have to know what you're dealing with before you can find the cure."

"What if there is no cure?" she asked, voicing a fear she hadn't allowed herself to consider.

"Even if there isn't a cure, there have to be ways to make the symptoms better. You're dealing with a disorder. There are treatments. You have options. We just have to find the best one."

She heard the pecking of his fingers on a keyboard on the other end. He was researching. He was looking for answers. Instead of judging her or backing away when she told him what she was up against, he was stepping up to help her find the way. He was doing what she'd known he would do, despite the voice in her mind warning her that he would turn and run.

She really had to stop listening to that voice. That was the voice that had stopped her from admitting to Tobias how dark her world became every June when she was faced with Katie's birthday and the anniversary of her death. That voice had told her she wasn't worthy of Tobias and all the love he'd showered her with. That voice had convinced her to fake her way through his attempts at getting her help over the years.

She still had the same fear that she was going to be rejected for not being perfect. A fear her father had unwittingly embedded so deep in her psyche, she didn't know how she'd ever overcome it, even with the help of a qualified professional.

"I knew," she admitted as he continued to type. "I've known for a long time that something was wrong. I would joke about how good I was at shutting down, but I never gave the issue any real thought, you know?"

"That kind of denial isn't uncommon, sweetheart. Many of us know we have a problem and choose to pretend that acknowledging it means we're somehow in control."

"Simon?" she asked when he grew quiet, likely reading whatever report he'd found.

"Hmm?"

Carol swallowed hard. "You're the only person I've told. I mean, I've told some family and friends that I'm seeing a counselor, but you're the only one I've told about the diagnosis. I don't know why, but I'm not ready for anyone else to know that."

"Thank you for telling me. For trusting me."

She hesitated before admitting, "I do trust you. I really do. That's not easy for me."

"I promise you won't regret opening up to me. I'm going to be here for whatever you need. Do you want help figuring out the next step?"

With that one question, a weight was lifted from her chest. She was able to take a breath. To think. To look at the next step and not feel so overwhelmed.

# ELEVEN

CAROL SLIPPED her tennis shoes on as she narrowed her eyes at her mother. "Are you wearing makeup?" She hadn't seen her mom with blush and lipstick on in years, but the telltale signs of pink were obvious.

Judith rolled her shoulders back in the way she did before digging her heels in. "I'm allowed."

"I didn't say you weren't," Carol responded. "I'm surprised. That's all." She turned toward her aunt, who was pulling on a sweater. Ellen winked at her with a glimmer of her usual mischievousness. There was something amiss, but Carol couldn't pinpoint what. An undercurrent between Judith and Ellen implied secrets Carol didn't know.

"Are we going?" Judith asked.

"We're going," Ellen said.

As they walked out into the morning sunshine, Carol grabbed Ellen's arm and pulled her back a few steps. "What's with her?" she asked her aunt.

"I can't tell you. She made me promise."

Carol tilted her head and narrowed her eyes. "Aunt Ellen."

Ellen made the motion of zipping her lips, locking them, and tossing away the key. "You're a smart kid. You'll figure everything out soon enough."

Carol wanted to press but knew better. Her aunt was clearly enjoying the game, whatever it was, and looking forward to seeing Carol catch on. Walking between the two older women, Carol tried to put the puzzle together as they made their way toward the community center of the retirement community.

The last time she'd visited her mom, they hadn't stepped foot in the center. This would be the second time since Carol had arrived a few days prior. She guessed her mom and aunt were more settled in now, more open to connecting with their neighbors, since they were so determined to go to the neighborhood holiday party. But then Carol thought about her mom's makeup and how she'd taken her time styling her hair into her signature bun. The sweater she wore adorned with a butterfly-shaped brooch decorated with colorful gems. Carol remembered her grandmother wearing the pin years and years ago. Her mother had only worn it for special occasions—especially when she was trying to impress someone.

She managed to contain the gasp, but she couldn't stop herself from gawking at her mother with wide eyes and a gaping mouth. Jerking her head to her aunt, the same shock on her face, Carol discreetly pointed to her mom and mouthed, *Is she...*

Ellen snickered and gently nudged Carol.

"I can see you two," Judith snapped. "I'm not blind."

"*Mom*," Carol said with all the astonishment she was feeling. Focusing on the woman who had been too stuck up for her own good most of her life, Carol tried to control her smile. "Do you have a boyfriend?"

Judith frowned at Carol but outright glared at Ellen when she laughed. "Stop it."

"I didn't do anything," Ellen said, even though she was giggling.

Carol forced her grin away as she gave her mother a stern frown. "I hope you remember what you told me when I started dating John."

"Caroline," Judith warned.

Leveling her eyes at her mother, Carol said, "Men are only after *one* thing."

"Don't give away the milk before you sell the cow," Ellen said.

Carol's faux sternness gave way as she laughed at her aunt's advice.

Judith clearly wasn't amused. "You're both juvenile," she stated as she continued walking. "I'm not dating anyone. I'm too old for that."

"Too old my ass. You've got a pulse, don't you?" Ellen asked.

"Barely," Judith countered. "Leonard is a very nice man.

He's a good friend. We enjoy each other's company, but that's all."

Carol heard echoes of herself in that statement. Hadn't she said that about Simon repeatedly? Rather than continue to tease her mom, Carol backed off, the way she had insisted Lara do. "That's good, Mom. I'm glad you found a new friend."

"Thank you," Judith said.

They finished the walk talking about anything other than Leonard or the fact that Judith had primped before meeting her *friend*. Once they walked inside, though, Ellen nudged Carol and nodded toward a silver-haired man making his way toward them with a big grin on his face. Slightly hunched, he scooted along with the help of a walker.

*Slide, step, step.*

*Slide, step, step.*

His smile never eased once.

When the man finally reached the women, he took Carol's hand without hesitation. However, he didn't shake it in a greeting. He wrapped both hands around hers and clutched her fingers like they were old friends themselves.

"You look so much like your mother," he said with a tender smile. "She talks about you all the time, Carol."

A few months ago, the comparison between her and her mother would have made Carol cringe. Now that she and her mom were on better terms, the idea of being a younger version of Judith Stewart wasn't nearly as offensive. Carol thanked him, ready to make small talk to get to know him a little, but he dropped her hand like a hot potato and turned to Judith. The moment he focused on her, Carol may as well have disappeared. Within moments, Judith and Leonard were walking away without another word.

Ellen put her arm around Carol's waist. "Nope. Nothing happening there."

"Oh my God," Carol muttered. "They're adorable."

"Oh, honey, don't let your mother hear you say that. She'll never tolerate being called adorable."

Carol chuckled, mostly because her aunt was right. "I guess you're stuck with me."

"I could do worse, kiddo. How about a game of checkers?"

"Sounds like a plan." As they walked to an empty table, Carol glanced at her mom and her heart nearly melted. She'd never seen her mom happy. Not *really* happy. Judith had suffered from depression most of Carol's life. Carol had grown up being kept at arm's length from her parents and feeling like a burden. Only recently had she realized how hard her mom had worked to keep putting one foot in front of the other. For decades, Carol had resented how she'd been raised. Now she could see how hard her mom had been fighting her own demons. Seeing Judith smile almost brought tears to Carol's eyes.

She hoped whatever was happening between Judith and Leonard kept growing and making her mom smile like that. She deserved to be happy after all these years. Even if her mom was in her midseventies, she deserved happiness, love, and—if Carol was interpreting the exchange correctly— someone to flirt with.

"When did this start?" Carol asked her aunt as they settled in to play a game.

"A few weeks ago. Don't worry," Ellen said, sliding the red checkers to Carol while she kept the black for herself. "I've already had your cousins research him on the Internet. He's clean."

Carol chuckled as she put her pieces on the board. "That's good. I'm sure they were thorough."

Ellen moved one of her checkers first without any debate as to who would take the first turn. "Would you like them to look into Simon?"

Sliding a red plastic disk forward, she glanced at her aunt. "No. I've known Simon for over twenty-five years. I feel pretty confident I can trust him."

"There were a lot of years when you weren't in contact. Maybe you don't know him as well as you think."

Carol grinned. "He's the chief of staff at a prestigious children's hospital. I'm quite confident they wouldn't have given him that position if there were skeletons in his closet."

"Oh, honey. You can't be that naive."

Carol couldn't really explain why, but her defenses spiked. She knew Ellen meant well, but any insinuation that Simon might harbor some kind of ill intent made her want to protect him. She didn't. She simply stated, "Simon's a good man. No background search required. Thank you, though."

Ellen seemed satisfied. For a moment. Then she smirked that same mischievous grin she'd had when she was waiting for Carol to figure out that Judith had a *friend*. "You do realize that you said a background check wasn't necessary because you trust him, not because you aren't interested in dating him."

Carol opened her mouth, but her aunt's know-it-all grin made her stop short of explaining herself. Much like with Lara and Mary, even Elijah, the more she insisted she wasn't interested in dating, the less Ellen would believe her. Instead, she shook her head. "I really don't know why everyone is trying to pair me off."

"Because it's time."

"Don't you think that's my decision to make?"

Ellen tilted her head, and the teasing light in her eyes faded. "Look around you, honey. You're too young to set yourself up for a future like this."

Carol didn't have to scan the room. She knew what her aunt was implying. If she didn't pick up the pieces and move on soon, she might never pick them up. What was left of her life would pass by, leaving her a lonely widow in a retirement community. Her aunt didn't have to say that. Carol had already considered the possibility. "I've been a widow for a little over a year. I'd like to take some time to finish grieving before throwing myself at the first unsuspecting male who comes along."

Ellen pressed her lips into a thin line. She might have been trying to bite back whatever she was thinking, but Carol knew her well enough to know she was going to share her thoughts, no matter how much a voice in the back of her mind warned her not to. Ellen and Judith had a way of saying whatever the hell they wanted.

"Do you want to know why everyone is so concerned about you, Carol?" Ellen asked.

"Because my husband is dead and I'm spending my life driving around the country in an RV alone?"

"No. Well, that's not all of it anyway." Ellen pointed at her niece. "You've spent your entire life hiding away from what hurts you. You shut down, put your head in the sand, and pretend your pain doesn't exist. We don't want to see you doing that again."

"King me," Carol said after moving one of her pieces.

Ellen frowned as she stacked one circle on top of another.

Carol sat back and drew a breath. Simon had encouraged her to open up to her mom and aunt about her diagnosis. Here, once again, was a segue that she could take. She considered doing so for a heartbeat, but when she spoke, she said, "I'm aware of my ability to shut down, Aunt Ellen. That's something I'm trying to change. I'm in therapy now. I'm pushing myself to do the things that scare me. Or have you forgotten the episode at the pool?"

"I haven't forgotten anything. We're all proud of the steps you've been taking. Your mom can sleep a little easier knowing you're talking to someone. But what if you're on the road, alone, and decide to stuff all your hurt into a bottle? There won't be anyone there to push you to let your pain out. You're going to cause yourself some real damage. That's the same thing we feared when you left Dayton after Katie died. You shut everyone out and moved away, and none of us could help you. You're doing that again."

Carol shook her head. She'd taken Katie's urn and left

Dayton without a word because she couldn't be in their house, surrounded by the things that constantly reminded her that Katie was gone. She couldn't stay married to the man she blamed for taking her daughter. She'd had to leave because her rage toward John had terrified her.

"This isn't the same," Carol said, forcing those decades-old hurt from her mind. "I know I'm not alone now. I know I have family and friends to help me."

"I'm glad you know that. I hope you're using the support you have."

Sitting back in her chair, Carol eyed her aunt. "You know, I have an entire life of bad habits to break. Tobias spent most of our marriage trying to coax me into finding better ways to cope, but I wasn't ready. Losing him made me retract in a way I hadn't since Katie died. I would have been perfectly content to stay that way. I'm so used to slipping inside myself that I don't even realize I'm fading sometimes."

"Well, we see it," Ellen stated.

"I am getting better at recognizing the cycle and pulling myself free before I sink too low. I understand that you all are worried," Carol said, "but I am reaching out now, even when it's uncomfortable. Have you forgotten my last visit? I was here for the sole purpose of connecting with Mom. I was here to fix our relationship and bring us closer. I'm here now because we *are* closer. I spent Thanksgiving with my in-laws. I'm *not* shutting people out."

Aunt Ellen put her hand on Carol's. "We all love you so much. We want you to be happy, whatever that looks like now."

"I know."

"But do you know you *can* be happy again? All you have to do is give yourself permission, Carol. Just allow yourself to be happy."

Carol glanced to where her mom and her new friend were sitting. Much like Carol and Ellen, the game they'd sat down to play was forgotten as conversation became the main focus. The difference was that Judith was beaming. Her smile was bright, something Carol couldn't ever recall seeing on her mother's face.

Carol wanted that too. She missed having that. She suspected that if she called Simon right now and told him she might want to try again, he'd agree. He hadn't said as much, but the connection between them seemed to be as strong now as it had been all those years ago.

All she had to do was open herself up to it. To him.

That was definitely easier said than done.

———

*Dread settled in Carol's gut the moment her plane touched down in Houston. That sensation grew with each mile her friend drove, taking her closer to home. Carol had spent the last two weeks in St. Louis with her in-laws. She hadn't been home since Elijah had driven her and Mary back to St. Louis for Tobias's funeral. She hadn't been home alone since she'd lost him.*

*Tears filled her eyes, but her dark sunglasses hid them long enough to blink them away before they could fall.*

"Doing okay?" Alyssa asked, as if she sensed Carol's inner turmoil.

"Mm-hmm."

She reached across the console and took Carol's hand. "You can stay with me if you want."

"Thanks, but I'll be okay. And thanks for picking me up from the airport." She opened her mouth, about to ask if she'd already said that. She couldn't remember. Everything was still a blur. The world around her was going at a faster speed than her mind could process.

"I'm happy to help," Alyssa said before Carol could clarify. "You know..."

Though her mind was drifting in a fog, Carol sensed the inevitable onslaught of sympathy. Pity had a specific feel that Carol had come to know all too well. The heaviness, the tiptoeing into the conversation, the hesitancy to point out that Carol was a widow now.

"Don't," she said before the words could come out of Alyssa's mouth.

"Don't what?"

Heaving a sigh, Carol looked out at the scenery passing by. "Don't try to fix this. You can't."

"I wasn't going to try fix anything. I was going to tell you I'm here for you, no matter what you need or when you need it. I'm a phone call away."

"I'm aware of that."

Alyssa let a halfhearted laugh leave her. "Sure you are. But will you call me? No," she answered before Carol could. "You won't. We both know it."

"I called when I needed a ride, didn't I? I could have called any number of driving services, but I called you. My so-called best friend."

"So-called," Alyssa muttered as she squeezed Carol's hand. "I am your best friend, and as your best friend, I think I'm allowed to tell you that I'm worried about you. Come home with me."

Carol shook her head. "No."

"I don't think you're ready to be in that house, Carol."

The words stung. For some reason, that house sounded cold. Cruel. A bubble of anger rose in Carol's chest, and she had to forcibly swallow to push the feeling down. The urge to lash out was illogical. Alyssa would never be cruel; she'd never be mean. Alyssa's words hadn't angered Carol, but rather, the reality— her friend had dared to vocalize Carol's own fears.

Carol wasn't ready to be in that house. She wasn't ready to go home, to face the world she'd built with a husband who was no longer there. Tobias was gone. All that remained was that house and a million memories that she'd cherish forever.

"I can't hide forever," Carol managed to say, though her voice was strained.

"No, but you don't have to go home today either. You just got back to town. Let's ease you into this."

Ease her into this? She almost laughed. She'd been slammed into "this" as hard as Tobias had been slammed by a truck. The only difference was that her injuries weren't going to kill her. No. She'd live with this pain for the rest of her life. "I've been gone for two weeks," she said flatly. "It's time for me to go home."

Alyssa took the next exit, the one that would lead to Carol's neighborhood. The one that would take her to an empty house *where she wouldn't be able to escape the quiet emptiness. Where she would have to pack up the clothes he'd never wear again. The books he'd never read again. Take care of the flowers he'd never again coax into blooming.*

*Sinking her teeth into her lip, Carol bit until she tasted blood. The metallic taste on her tongue and the pain on her flesh was enough to stop the sob from rising in her chest and escaping. Swallowing hard, she took a slow, deep breath. She had to hold herself together for a little bit longer.*

*Within minutes, Alyssa turned into the driveway of the two-story home Carol and Tobias had bought fifteen years prior.*

*The trepidation in Carol's heart dropped to the pit of her stomach, but she ignored the sensation as she put herself into autopilot. "Thanks for the ride," she said, reaching for the door handle.*

*"I can come in—"*

*"No." She climbed out and opened the back door to get her suitcase. She offered Alyssa a weak smile. "I love you, and I appreciate what you're trying to do, but I have to handle this one alone."*

*"I don't think you should, Carol," Alyssa said quietly.*

*"I'll check in with you later."*

*Something like fear touched Alyssa's eyes. "You know that I love you, right?"*

*A slight laugh left Carol. "I'm not going to do anything stupid, Lys. I need some time to melt down on my own, okay? I haven't had a minute alone. I need that."*

*"I don't want to leave you."*

"Well," Carol said, "I'm not giving you a choice. Thanks for the ride."

She pulled her suitcase from the back seat and shut the door. After she punched the security code into a panel, the garage door slid up. Carol was instantly met with Tobias's car parked next to hers. She disregarded the pang because she refused to give her friend any more cause to be concerned. Once inside the garage, she pushed a button to close the door and headed for the kitchen entrance.

As soon as the automatic door closed, blocking Alyssa's view of her, Carol choked out a sob and stopped her forward movement. Putting her hand on the hood of Tobias's car, she took several gasping breaths as her strength waned.

She was home for the first time since leaving for his funeral.

She was empty for the first time since he'd smiled at her so many years ago.

Come on in, the house seemed to say. Take a nice long look at the life you'll never get back.

At the door between the garage and the kitchen, Carol hesitated. She stood there for what seemed like hours before finally pushing the door open and taking one step into the kitchen. From the doorway, she scanned from the kitchen to the open living area, through the sliding glass doors where his flowers were dancing in the breeze.

Everything was the same, but everything was different.

The quiet that met her when she came home was deafening now. The silence ran deeper. As she stood there, she recalled the first time she went home after Katie had died. The first time she'd walked into that house with the understanding that her daughter would never come home again.

The space that she'd been so familiar with all those years ago was foreign in that moment, just like how the home she'd shared with Tobias for fifteen years was foreign now. A land where she didn't belong. A place she'd never been to before, one where she didn't want to stay.

Dropping her suitcase at her feet, she again looked around the open layout, more slowly this time, really taking in her home, from the granite countertops to the stainless steel appliances. The white furniture and the metal and glass coffee table Tobias had shipped in from Italy.

"Hey," a soft voice called from behind her.

Carol jolted and slowly turned to where Alyssa stood a few feet behind her.

She lifted the bag she was holding. "I grabbed us something to eat."

The words slowly sank in, and Carol creased her brow. "When did you do that?"

"After I dropped you off," Alyssa said. "Have you... Have you been standing here all this time?"

All this time? Carol had no idea how much time Alyssa meant, but the deli where she'd picked up their dinner rarely took fewer than twenty minutes to fill an order. Had Carol been standing in the doorway of her kitchen for twenty minutes? She couldn't really say.

Alyssa pushed her way into the house, forcing Carol to take a few steps deeper into the kitchen. As Carol watched, feeling once again that she was outside her body, Alyssa pulled two *plates from the cabinet and got silverware. Then she filled two wineglasses with a pinot grigio as she mumbled about not knowing what wine went with white bean and tuna salad but she guessed that didn't really matter.*

*"Come on," Alyssa said after setting two plates on the counter. "Sit."*

*Carol looked at the place settings in front of the stools she and Tobias used when they didn't want to bother sitting at the table. A tear welled in her eye and dripped down her cheek. "I hate him," she whispered.*

*Alyssa stopped moving, as if finally realizing she was about to get the emotional outburst she'd been asking for since picking Carol up.*

*"That son of a bitch. What was he doing?" Carol furrowed her brow as she watched her friend. "What the hell was he doing running with the traffic? In the fog? He knew better. He knew better!" Carol ground her teeth, trying to stifle the anger at Tobias that was suddenly boiling. "You run against the traffic. You run so you can see what is coming at you. What the fuck was he doing?"*

*Furious, Carol reached for one of the plates Alyssa had set out.*

*"No," Alyssa stated. "That's our lunch, and I am starving." She held out the bottle of wine. "Throw this. It's not that great."*

*Carol stared at the bottle before sighing. "What's wrong with it?"*

*Alyssa smacked her lips and scrunched up her face. "It's got this really weird aftertaste. I don't know what is."*

*"That was expensive."*

*"Well, it's terrible." She pushed the bottle toward Carol. "Throw it."*

*Another tear slid unacknowledged down Carol's cheek. "No. It'll leave a mess. I don't want to clean up." Dropping onto a stool, Carol sniffed.*

*"Potholes," Alyssa said. When Carol lifted her face to her, she offered a soft smile. "That stretch of road where he was hasn't been fixed yet. He was running with traffic to avoid the potholes."*

*Carol recalled how the street had been due for repair since winter. "Oh. Right. Potholes." Leaning her elbows on the table, Carol rested her forehead against her palms. "He was trying to avoid breaking an ankle. Instead, he got a broken back and a fractured skull. Oh my God." Despite her tears and her anger, a laugh built in her chest until she let the sound loose. "Oh my God. He's dead because he didn't want to trip."*

*Leaning back, Carol looked at her friend. Alyssa didn't seem to see the humor in that. She wasn't laughing. Carol swallowed down was left of her chuckles and blew out a breath.*

*"You need this," Alyssa said, holding out the wine she'd been drinking. "Even if it does taste like rotten feet."*

*Carol didn't argue. She couldn't. She accepted the glass and drank down what was left in one gulp.*

———

Carol opened her eyes, and anxiety immediately filled her. Christmas morning. Oh, how she hated Christmas morning. She tried to stop the memories, but they steamrolled her. In her mind, she heard footsteps tiptoeing into her room. She felt a few gentle tugs right before Katie whispered, "Mama. Mama, wake up. Santa came."

Carol kicked the blankets off and rolled to sit before the pain could take hold. Not this year. She wasn't going to dwell on the hurt this year. Her mom had said several times how much she was looking forward to this Christmas. Carol wasn't going to let the sadness ruin this day for them. She pushed thoughts of Katie and Tobias from her mind, as far as she could.

Picking up the framed photo her mom had given her a few days prior, Carol stared at Katie's smiling face. "Merry Christmas, baby," she whispered.

She was distracted when the bedroom door opened. Her aunt Ellen poked her head in and offered Carol a big smile.

"Morning," Ellen said.

Carol set the picture aside. "Morning."

Ellen shuffled in and wrapped an arm around Carol's shoulder as she sat. After kissing her cheek, Ellen said, "You feel whatever you need to feel today. I'll keep your mom distracted if you need me to."

Carol sighed. "Thanks. I'm going to try really hard to get through. Today is important to Mom."

"It's important to all of us. I can't remember the last time we were all together for a holiday, but that doesn't discount how difficult today is for you."

Carol patted her aunt's knee. "I appreciate that. You know what will make the day better?"

"Coffee?"

"Coffee."

"It's ready, sweetheart," Ellen said and then kissed Carol's cheek. "I'll pour you a cup as soon as you pull me up off this couch."

Carol laughed as she stood, pulling Ellen with her. "I don't know why you keep this thing. It's so uncomfortable."

"It's red."

Apparently that was all the reason her aunt needed. For now, Carol was willing to let that be enough. If having an uncomfortable red sofa made her aunt happy, that was enough.

"I'll be there in a minute," Carol said as she crossed the hall to the bathroom. She needed to brush her teeth and finish waking up before she started this day.

When she finally made her way to the kitchen, her aunt had already poured her a mug and her mom was putting pancakes and two slices of bacon onto a plate. Once again, Carol focused on pushing away the looming depression and kissed her mom's cheek.

"Eat up," Judith said. "Then we'll open presents."

"Thanks," Carol said, sitting at the table.

She waited for the other two women to join her before she started eating. Despite her attempts at being present, the past pulled her in a thousand different directions. Childhood Christmases filled with fear and disappointment. Katie laughing and chatting excitedly. Tobias spoiling Carol with gifts and promises of a future that was ripped away.

She didn't even realize the thoughts had consumed her

until her aunt rubbed her back. She took the plate of half-eaten food from Carol.

Blinking, Carol offered her mom a weak smile. "Sorry. I guess I faded."

"It's okay," Judith assured her.

Carol sipped her coffee, surprised to find her drink had cooled to a few degrees above room temperature. Damn it. She'd separated her mind from her body so she didn't have to feel again. The temptation to confess she'd been diagnosed with PTSD was almost overwhelming, but then her mom let out a breath and sadness touched her eyes.

Rather than add to the disappointment on her mom's face, Carol grabbed Judith's hand and forced a smile. "Are you ready to open presents?"

Her mom nodded, and they carried what was left of their breakfast dishes to the sink. Shuffling into the living room, Carol went right to the tree to get gifts for her mom and aunt that she'd bought while on the road. They'd made an agreement prior to the holiday that they were giving one gift per person because none of them needed anything and Carol didn't have storage in the RV for anything nonessential.

Sitting on the floor in front of them, she snapped a few pictures as they opened the gift bags.

Ellen gasped when she held up the handmade coffee mug stamped with a recreation of petroglyphs at a site in New Mexico. "This is beautiful, Carol. Thank you."

"As soon as I saw that, I knew you had to have it."

"Is that what you thought about me when you found this?" Judith asked, holding up her gift.

Carol and Ellen laughed as Judith scowled at the bottle of margarita mix. Not too long ago, Carol had learned her mother's aversion to the mixed drink wasn't the taste as much as her reaction to the alcohol. Apparently her mom got a little unhinged when drinking tequila.

"It's a joke, Mom," Carol said when Judith continued to look displeased. "There's more in the bag."

Judith shoved the bottle at Ellen, who happily accepted the mix so she could look over the label.

"Oh," Ellen said. "This is exotic."

"Not really. It's from Arizona."

"Which makes it exotic," Ellen insisted.

Judith pulled a small jewelry box from the gift bag and lifted the top off. Her scowl softened as her lip trembled.

"Do you like it?" Carol ask when her mom simply stared.

Judith nodded. "It's lovely, Carol." She pulled the necklace out and held the sterling silver up to show Ellen the two rings forever entwined and the card that spoke of how the love of a mother and daughter would never be broken.

Carol had bought the necklace shortly after her last visit to Florida, when she and Judith had made amends after years of barely tolerating each other. Pushing herself up off the floor, she helped her mom put the necklace on and then kissed her cheek.

"Love you, Mom."

Judith put her hand on Carol's cheek. "I love you. I'm so happy you're here."

"Me too."

"Your turn, Carol," Ellen announced. "Get the tall box from behind the tree."

Carol crossed the room and snagged the box with her name on it. Though the box was tall and thin, she was quite certain of what was inside. Her aunt always sent art of some kind. That was her thing. Carol suspected she would find a painting. Tearing the paper back, she lifted the top off the box and found a ten-by-twenty-inch frame inside. Carefully sliding the canvas painting out, she gasped.

Her aunt was an amazing artist who usually stuck with abstracts to express herself. However, the image she'd made with acrylics looked like a photograph. Not just any photo—the painting was an exact replica of the backyard garden Tobias had so lovingly cared for. The garden that Carol had such a hard time letting go of when she'd sold their house.

So much for not crying on Christmas. The tears welled and fell before she could stop them. "Aunt Ellen," she choked out, "this is beautiful. Thank you so much. I love it."

"I hope the frame is small enough for you to find a place ·in the RV. If not, you can hang it here."

"I know exactly where to put it," Carol said and then sniffed as she accepted a tissue from her mom. After wiping her eyes, she tucked the painting back into the box to protect the acrylic until she could hang it in the RV.

"Well, I'm glad I gave you my gift the other day," Judith said, blinking her eyes dry, "or we'd all be a mess."

"Yeah," Carol agreed. "That would have pushed me over the edge."

Judith squeezed Carol's hand. "Even with the parts of us

that are missing, this has already been the best Christmas I've had in over twenty years."

Carol smiled as she hugged her mom. "I'm glad. It's better than I expected." Her mom's smile slipped, and Carol quickly added, "Because I thought I'd be miserable. I'm sad but not miserable. Thank you both for that. I have one more gift. It's for all of us."

Grabbing a box that she'd tucked discreetly behind a chair, she held it up and showed her mom and aunt. "A five-thousand-piece puzzle of the Salt Lake City skyline. This thing is going to take us *years* to finish."

Ellen clapped her hands excitedly, but Judith let out one of her dramatic sighs. She didn't care for puzzles nearly as much as her sister and daughter.

# TWELVE

CAROL WAS REFILLING her wineglass when the phone in her pocket rang. She'd already talked to all her in-laws, so the caller was either Alyssa or Simon. She bet on Simon before she even dug for the device. Seeing his name on the screen made her smile.

"Merry Christmas," she said as she pushed the wine stopper into the neck of the bottle. She didn't know why she bothered since she was pretty sure she'd finish the cabernet before the end of the night. Though her day had been better than anticipated, she was still doing whatever she needed to keep the depression lurking in the back of her mind at bay. Right now, that involved finishing the bottle that had been opened for dinner.

"Merry Christmas," Simon answered. "How was your day?"

She leaned against the counter. "Oh. You know."

"Another tough one?"

"Yeah," she said softly and then took a sip of her drink. "It was all right. But...well...you know."

"I know," he said with an underlying sympathetic tone.

Grabbing the bottle, she headed toward the room that she'd claimed for the duration of her visit with her mom and aunt. "How was yours?" she asked.

"Quiet. The girls were here for about an hour and then rushed off to do whatever college-aged kids do."

"Hanging out with friends, no doubt," Carol offered as she closed the door to the guest room. "Did you go anywhere? See some friends or anything?"

"No. I did binge-watch some TV shows that have been on my DVR for too long, though."

Carol sank down onto the big red sofa. "Sounds like a nice, quiet day."

"It was boring."

Something in his voice made Carol sit a bit taller. This wasn't the first time she'd heard something akin to loneliness reverberate around their talks. "Now that your kids are older, maybe you should reach out to friends to celebrate the holidays. You can't be the only one doing this empty-nest thing."

"I'm not. I have friends going through the same thing."

"So, plan a Christmas dinner at your place next year. Tobias and I had a holiday dinner every year for friends who didn't have family in Houston. Spending time with friends gave the day more meaning."

Simon was quiet for a few moments. "I'm not going to be here next Christmas."

She smirked. "Going to finally turn in that letter of resignation?"

Again, he was too hesitant in answering. Something was wrong.

"Simon?" she pressed. "Is everything okay?"

"Can I be honest with you about something?"

Her heart dropped to the bottom of her stomach. "Sure."

"I think I'm having a midlife crisis," he said.

The beginnings of a chuckle slipped from Carol's lips before she could stop herself. She abruptly pressed her fingertips to her mouth so she didn't outright laugh. "I'm sorry," she said. "I was expecting you to say something else."

"Like what?"

"I don't know," she admitted, "but not...*that*." Guilt tugged at her gut when he didn't respond. "What's going on?"

He exhaled loudly. "Well, I have everything I could possibly want, yet I had a miserable Christmas. I feel a like a secondhand shoe with my kids. I have a great career, a beautiful home, an amazing vacation house in the mountains, but I've spent so much of my time working for those things, I don't have anyone to share them with. What's the point in having things when you're the only one who's ever around to see them?"

Carol leaned back on the sofa and rubbed her forehead. "Holidays really exacerbate the loneliness, don't they?"

"Yeah," he said so quietly, she barely heard the word. "The last thing you need is to listen to my problems. Let's talk about something else."

"You listen to my problems all the time."

"Your problems are a little bit bigger than mine."

Even though he couldn't see her, Carol shook her head hard to show her disagreement. "No. They're different but no more valid than yours. Depression spikes around the holidays for a reason. Your kids are grown now. I imagine Christmas is vastly different than you're used to. That's hard, Simon. I'm sure you miss the way things used to be."

"I miss *you*," he blurted out.

The silence between them was heavy.

Carol licked her lips before saying, "I know."

"I don't think you do," he countered.

"Simon," she stated before he said too much. Her heart pounded in her chest as she lowered her defenses. "*I know*. I miss you too."

"Probably not the same way."

Carol had known this conversation was inevitable from the day his occasional check-ins had turned into almost daily calls. She'd seen this coming a mile away. She'd even warned Simon she wasn't ready for where this was headed. Yet, she hadn't stopped them from going in this direction, and she couldn't pretend that she didn't know why. Twenty-four years may have gone by, but being with Simon was as easy for her now as it had been back then. He had the kind of calm she'd lost when Tobias had died. The kind of calm she needed more than anything right now.

She ground her teeth, trying to stop herself from saying what she was thinking, but the words won. They slipped out for him to hear. "This thing...it's the same as it's always been. I'm falling apart, and you're here trying to put me back together. Just like all those years ago, there's a part of me begging me to run to you."

"I like that part of you," he said. "You should listen to that part."

A smile pulled at her lips. "I've been tempted, but I have to be careful. For both our sakes. Running to you would be so easy. Being with you has been easy from the day we met."

"Because we're good together, Caroline."

She closed her eyes. "Being good together didn't make our relationship right twenty-four years ago, and it doesn't make a relationship right today. I have too much to work through before I can even think about starting something new. I'm a big steaming pile of emotional mess right now. You deserve better than that."

He chuckled. "You're my favorite big steaming pile of emotional mess."

Carol laughed softly. "But you deserve better. I couldn't give all of myself to you then, and I certainly can't right now. That's not fair."

He was quiet for a few seconds. "I'm sorry. I'm pushing again."

"You don't have to push, Simon. You never did. I could show up at your door like I did before. You'd take me in and make me feel better. I think we'd be happy together."

"I *know* we would."

"No. Until I get my head on straight, part of me would be looking back instead of looking forward with you. Part of me would be holding back, too scared to let you in. I don't want to do that to you. I need time. I'm not asking you to wait—"

"But I would. I *am*. As soon as I saw you in Ohio a few months ago, I knew that if you were willing to try again, I was willing to wait until you were ready. One smile and I was smitten, just like back then."

Carol grinned slightly. "Well, I have a pretty great smile."

"You do. I think it's that little dimple in your right cheek that gets me."

"Okay," she stated. "Leave my dimple out of this." Carol finished the wine in her glass and looked at the bottle she'd carried with her. Rather than pour another drink, she set the glass aside. Her thoughts were swirling enough already. She had a million things she wanted to say to him. "I just got a formal diagnosis, Simon. I have to figure out how to tackle this thing. I need to do that before I insert myself into your life."

"You're already in my life."

Closing her eyes, she frowned. "That's not what I meant."

"I know what you meant."

"If we do this, we have to do it right this time," she said softly. "I can't go into another relationship with you knowing I'm not ready to give you my all."

"I understand," he said, but he sounded disappointed.

The urge to bend to please him was strong, but she resisted. She had to squeeze her eyes shut and grind her teeth, but she managed to not give in. "If you need to move on—"

"No," he said. "I'm still not going anywhere. Even if this never grows into more than a few phone calls a week to check in, I'm okay with that. I just don't want to lose you again."

"Simon," she whispered, "I don't want to give you the short end this time."

"You never gave me the short end. You gave what you could. I got greedy. And I'm going to again as soon as you give me permission."

Sinking down into the couch, Carol looked at the painting of the carefree woman that had connected with something inside her. Inhaling slowly, working up the courage, she finally said, "I'll give you permission. When I'm ready."

"First things first," Simon said after a few moments. "I'm going to turn in my letter of resignation and help the board find a suitable replacement while you work toward healing," he said in that take-charge tone she was so familiar with. "After that, I'll sell my house and move to Missouri. When you're ready, I hope you'll join me. In the meantime, I'm going to be in Missouri through the New Year. I would like to see you there."

She chuckled. "You're still persistent."

"You love that about me."

She loved a lot of things about him but opted to not voice them. Instead, she said, "Okay. First things first."

The idea of having something to work toward, a goal to reach, felt right. Knowing that goal was a future, possibly with Simon, was better.

"So, um," she started. "Did the girls like their presents?"

Though she'd instigated the topic change, she only half

listened as he told her how his daughters had loved the clothes Carol had helped him pick out online one evening. The rest of her mind was processing the reality that she'd taken the first real steps to moving on from her life with Tobias.

———

*There were times when Carol was tempted to pinch herself. Sitting with Tobias at a little café in Paris was definitely one of those times. This was their third trip to Europe, and she still couldn't believe this was her life. All the things she'd ever dreamed of for herself had come to pass. Almost all. She hadn't had the family she'd wanted, but she had nieces, and over time, that had become enough.*

*More than anything, she had an amazing husband who had helped her live the most fulfilling life she could have ever imagined having after losing Katie.*

*She smiled at Tobias as he mispronounced a phrase with a terrible French accent. "You're going to get us kicked out of the country," she warned. "They're going to take our passports and never let us back after we serve jail time for disturbing the peace."*

*Tobias laughed as he set his language guide aside. Resting his arms on the table, he eyed her in the way that he did when he analyzed things. As much as he called her out for overthinking and picking things apart, he could be equally as guilty at times. This was one of them. His mind was rolling something around, over and over, and he was trying to decide if he should voice the thoughts.*

*"Are you thinking of an escape plan?" she asked.*

*He shook his head slowly. "I'm thinking about us. About all the things we've done and have planned to do."*

*"That's a whole lot of thinking."*

*He nodded. "Are you happy, Carol?"*

*"Yes," she answered without hesitation. "Are you happy, Tobias?"*

*Instead of answering, he pulled apart the layers of his question. "I don't mean right now. I don't mean in this moment. I mean...in this life. Are you happy with the life we've built?"*

*Setting her cup aside, she put her hand on his and held his gaze. "Yes. I am happy. I am happier than I ever thought I could be again. You did that for me. You healed me."*

*He brought her hand to his lips and kissed her knuckles. "There is nothing in this world more important to me than your happiness. I want you to know that."*

*Carol tilted her head as she stared into his dark eyes. "Where is this coming from?"*

*He shrugged as he gazed at her tenderly. "I don't ever want you to look back on our time together and wish we'd done something differently."*

*Pressing her palm to his cheek, she offered him a reassuring smile. "I wouldn't do anything different, Tobias. I love you, and I love the life we've built. There is nothing I would change."*

*Sadness shadowed his eyes. "We've had some hard times."*

*He didn't have to acknowledge those times more than he had. She knew he meant the children they'd never had. She knew he meant the bouts of depression that nearly consumed her every June when she was faced with Katie's birthday and the anniversary of her death.*

*They'd certainly had hard times, but they'd overcome them. Even when June yanked the rug out from under Carol every time summer rolled around, they recovered. They rebounded, stronger than they'd been before. Tobias was usually the driving force for that. If left up to Carol, they likely would have dwelled and ignored and pretended until the shadows overcame them. She'd never had the strength to fight back when life pushed her too hard. Thank God Tobias did.*

*Leaning closer, pulling his face to hers, she pressed her lips against his and then brushed their noses together. "I love you."*

*"I love you," he said, "and I meant what I said. There is absolutely nothing I want more than to know you're happy."*

*"I'm happy. I'm so happy, it's not even normal."*

*"Well," he said, sitting back with a sly smirk on his lips, "nothing about you is normal, babe."*

*Carol broke off a piece of her sugar puff and tossed the bit at him, chuckling when the pastry bounced off his forehead.*

———

The next morning, Carol sat her mom and aunt down at their little kitchen table with cups of tea. After the talk with Simon, she had to come clean to her family. If she was going to move on the way she insisted she wanted to, she had to suck it up and get her ass moving on.

So, over a cup of chamomile, she told her mom and aunt

what she'd told Simon days before. She had been diagnosed with PTSD.

"What does that mean?" Judith asked.

"That means I've had a lot of trauma in my life that I've never healed from." That was the simplest way she could explain. "One of the symptoms is how I separate myself from reality so I don't feel the pain."

"But this... You've always been like that," Judith said, sounding confused that this was actually a problem. "You always disconnected. Even before we lost Katie."

Carol looked into her cup. This was going to be the really uncomfortable part of the conversation. "Mom. We've talked before about how hard Dad was on me. How his expectations of me were unrealistic and how threatening he could be when I didn't live up to them. I don't think you realized how scared I was of him."

She focused on her mom in time to see Judith sit taller, the way she did when she was about to defend herself against some kind of accusation that might imply she wasn't perfect.

Carol pressed on in hopes of deflating the situation before the confrontation could start. "I grew up feeling like I was one wrong move away from him coming completely unglued and hurting me. Growing up with him was terrifying. All the time, Mom. Every day."

Judith's posture softened as guilt shone in her eyes. "We did this to you?" she asked quietly.

"No," Carol stated. However, her mom wasn't exactly wrong. Her father had never raised a hand to Carol, but he'd never had to. His brand of psychological abuse left scars she was only starting to understand. "This is how I learned how to cope with things that were too daunting for me to handle. Stepping back emotionally is a common defense mechanism that everyone has. I happen to use that tactic more often...and more effectively...than most people." Carol grinned. "You always did say I excelled where others were mediocre."

"Don't make jokes," Aunt Ellen said softly. "Not about this."

Carol frowned as she looked at her aunt—not because Aunt Ellen had warned her about making light of the situation but because the usual sign of mischief in her eyes was missing. Carol had stolen the happiness from her aunt's eyes. She hated that. She hated that she'd replaced Aunt Ellen's constant smile with obvious worry.

"I'm going to be okay," Carol told her aunt. She tapped into Simon's reassurances. "Now that we know what's wrong, we're going to find a way to fix what's broken. My doctor knows what she's dealing with now. We'll start working out a treatment plan after the New Year."

"Why *after* the New Year?" Judith asked. Her voice had taken that sharp turn that lit Carol's fuse, the judgmental tone that warned a fight was imminent. "Why are you waiting?"

Keeping her voice calm to counteract her mother's overreaction, Carol said, "Because I wanted to get through the holidays before delving too much deeper into all this."

"Carol—" Judith started.

"Mom, I want to take some time to process what's going on and breathe a little first. That's all."

"Stay here," Ellen all but begged. "Please don't try to sort through all this while you're on the road, Carol. You're going to need someone there to support you."

Carol nodded in agreement. "I'm not going to be alone. I'm heading back to Houston for a while."

"No," Judith said. She shook her head as if this were her decision. "You'll stay here."

"Mom," Carol said as evenly as possible. "I'm going back to Houston. I told you, Alyssa is having a hard time."

Pressing her lips together, Judith clearly tried but failed to keep her thoughts to herself. "If she's having a hard time, how is she going to help you through yours? You need to be with someone who can take care of you."

"I can take care of myself."

"But you don't," Judith snapped. "You never have."

Aunt Ellen lifted her hands in the way she did when she needed to intervene between mother and daughter. "Okay. Listen, Carol, we love you. We worry about you. We would both feel better if you were closer."

Taking her mom's hand, Carol sighed. "I understand. I appreciate that you want me here, but I have to start rebuilding my life. Part of that is working with my therapist to sort out whatever this issue is. I have a support system in Houston."

"Not a very good one," Judith stated. "Not if it took *John Bowman* to make you realize something was wrong."

Anytime Judith said Carol's ex-husband's name, she spit

out the words like poison. Carol thought they'd moved beyond Judith's resentments where John was concerned. Apparently not.

"Okay," Carol said with a flat but firm tone. "Mom, this is not going to dissolve into an argument. I shared this with you because I don't want to hide things from you. I want us to be open and honest with each other. You have to respect that I'm making decisions based on what is best for me. You can support me, or you can keep your thoughts to yourself. Those are your only two options."

"Carol," Aunt Ellen said in her mediator tone. "We're allowed to be worried about you."

"I'll be staying with Alyssa. If I need help, she will be there," Carol assured them. "She was my rock after Tobias's funeral."

Ellen frowned, but Judith was the one who stated what they were all thinking. "Need I remind you that you got arrested for taking a tire iron to the street after Tobias's funeral?"

"No," Carol said. "I remember. That wasn't Alyssa's fault."

"Well, where was she when you reached your breaking point?" Judith demanded.

"At her house. In bed, most likely. I said she would be there to help me, not lock me in a room." Carol stared at her mom for a moment. "Even if I stayed here, I wouldn't stay *here*," she said, gesturing around the kitchen. "I would get my own place. I'm not living with you."

Judith creased her brow. "Why not?"

"I love you, Mom," Carol stated firmly, "but we cannot live together."

Judith opened her mouth, but this time, Ellen gripped her hand.

Shaking her head, Aunt Ellen said, "Judy. You and Carol cannot live together. None of us would survive that."

"We're doing better," Judith stated.

"We are," Carol agreed, "and I'd like to keep things that way. I'll stay through the end of the week like I planned. Then I'm going back to Texas so I can start whatever plan my therapist sets up."

After one of her signature dramatic sighs, Judith frowned. "Fine. But if anything happens to you, this Alyssa person will hear from me."

Carol smirked. "I'll make sure she knows."

# THIRTEEN

SEVERAL DAYS LATER, Carol sank down into an Adirondack chair in Alyssa's backyard, happy to be off the road and happier to have her friend for company rather than her mother. The last few days with her mom had been tense. Carol realized belatedly that she should have saved the PTSD talk until after she'd left. Though she appreciated her mom and aunt worrying, they'd spent the last three days of her visit trying to convince her to stay. Her mom had even suggested they look for an apartment for her.

Being at Alyssa's was like breathing fresh air after being stuffed in a suitcase for days. Though the backyard faced the wrong direction for Carol to watch the sunset, the orange glow spreading across the sky was amazing. Stretching her legs out, Carol crossed them at the ankles as Alyssa rambled on excitedly.

"You know this isn't going to be like *Laverne & Shirley*, right?" Carol asked, referencing the television show they usually ended up watching when they had a girls' night in. The hijinks on the old show amused them endlessly.

"The hell it isn't," Alyssa stated. "I'm single now. We're getting into some things."

Carol smiled as she shook her head. She had no doubt Alyssa would try to get them into some things; she had many times in the past. However, Carol's level head tended to win out. "Did you hear what I said about starting treatment?"

"I did," Alyssa said, her tone softening to sound more supportive than mischievous. "Sweetie, I know this is something new and scary to you, but I've been in and out therapy all my life thanks to my crazy-ass mother. *Treatment* is a fancy word for medication and counseling sessions. You're going to be fine, and so am I, now that I've decided that I don't care if Jason divorces me."

Carol wished she could believe Alyssa's cheerful outlook. She was dreading whatever hidden disasters they both had waiting to be discovered as they continued working on their new lives. "I hope you're right."

"I am. Trust me. Now, listen."

Carol had heard that protective tone before from her best friend. This was the point when she tried to fix everything, which disappointed Carol. She didn't want someone swooping in to fix her life.

Alyssa held a wineglass in one hand and pointed at Carol with the other. "I'm going to take some vacation time to help you get settled and get back into a routine."

"That's not necessary," Carol said.

"Don't say that. I'm offering to help you. Your response is *thank you*."

Carol toasted her friend with her glass of rosé. "Thank you."

"I don't want you to worry about anything," Alyssa said with the same soft voice she'd used so often after Tobias had died. "I'm going to take care of you."

"I don't want that," Carol countered. "That's why I'm staying with *you*. If I wanted someone hovering over me, I would have stayed with my mother. I need time and space to sort through all this."

Alyssa blew out a raspberry. "Bullshit. You and I both know if someone isn't looking after you, you'll stick your head in the sand."

Though Carol couldn't blame everyone for assuming that was what she was going to do, she was getting tired of explaining herself. "The point of all this is so I stop doing that. I know this is odd to hear, but I don't need you pushing me, because I'm learning how to push myself. This entire thing has come about because I'm trying to work through my problems like a normal person instead of like…"

"Like you?"

Carol scoffed. "Yeah. Instead of like *me*. I have to learn how to face things on my own."

"You don't have to do it on your own, Carol. There is a happy medium."

"Maybe. But I've never been a middle-of-the-road kind of gal."

Alyssa toasted her. "I'm glad you're trying, but this

transformation to *Normal Carol* won't be easy. I'll be waiting in the wings when you need me."

Normal Carol? She had to laugh. She had no idea what "normal" was.

"I'm very glad you're taking steps to get help," Alyssa continued.

Focusing up at the sky, Carol bit at her lip for a few seconds. "Do you, um, do you remember when I told you about Simon Miller?"

"The doctor you used to shag?"

Carol instantly felt the warmth of a blush. "Yeah. That one."

"What about him?"

"We've been talking," Carol hesitantly admitted. "A lot. I saw him in St. Louis. We had dinner."

Alyssa gasped and sat taller. "What? Carol! Why didn't you tell me sooner?"

"Because it didn't seem right to tell you when you were dealing with your breakup."

Alyssa turned her lips into a disgruntled frown. "Divorce. Just say it. I'm dealing with my divorce. So, what's going on with you and Simon?"

Carol couldn't help but smile. "He told me he hopes we can try again. But I have no idea what I'm getting into, what's going to happen. He says he'll be here, whatever I need, but I don't want to drag him into this thing."

"This *thing*?" Alyssa repeated. "Carol, getting a diagnosis of any kind can be unsettling, but don't let this overwhelm you.

You have bad coping skills. You're going to learn new ones. You're going to take a long, hard look at all the shit in your life. The process will be tough. But you're going to be okay."

"I'm going to have to relive some really ugly things, and I don't know what that's going to do to me. What if... What if this doesn't get better?"

"Honey," Alyssa said softly, "you're never going to recover from the day Katie died. Not completely. What you went through was traumatic. You went through things a mother should never go through. Part of you will *always* be reliving that day. Part of you will *always* be trapped in that bad marriage with John. Part of you will *always* be walking into that hospital room and seeing Tobias. You'll never completely heal those wounds, but you do have to learn how to live with them."

"That's the plan," Carol whispered.

"Can I tell you something else? About Simon?"

Carol creased her brow. Alyssa had never met Simon. What could she possibly have to say about him? "I guess."

"If standing by you while you go through hell is too much for him, then he doesn't deserve you anyway," Alyssa said. "You'll never find another Tobias, but you will find someone who is strong enough and loves you enough to stand by you. No matter what."

Carol grinned at the protective undertones. "Simon wants to stand by me. I told him he has to wait."

Sitting forward, Alyssa looked at Carol like she'd lost her mind. "You told him *what*?"

"He was my savior once. I'm going to save myself this time."

"That man wants to help you through this, and you told him no?" Shaking her head, Alyssa sat back. "Good thing you found a therapist, Carol, because you *are* crazy."

———

*Caroline parked in the driveway of a little white two-story house. Simon's house. The place where he'd lived before moving to Dayton a year ago. When she'd gone to the hospital to quit her job, he'd pulled her aside and tried to comfort her.*

*He couldn't.*

*Katie was dead. How could he possibly make that better?*

*He'd done his best, though. He'd offered to do whatever he could to make things easier for her. That was when she told him she was leaving. She had no idea where she was going, but she couldn't stay with John. She couldn't stay in that house where Katie had lived her short life. She couldn't continue living her life as if Katie hadn't died.*

*Rather than beg her to stay, Simon understood her need to run away. He sent her to St. Louis. He told her to go straight to his real estate agent's office and get the keys to his house—the one he was trying to sell. He told her to stay there as long as she needed.*

*He gave her a place to go when she had nowhere else to turn.*

*She had a home, and thanks to Simon, she had the phone number of the head nurse at the hospital where he used to work. She had a lead on a job.*

*She had everything she could possibly need to start over.*

*Everything but her daughter.*

*Taking her suitcase and the small purple bag of Katie's belongings Caroline had packed before leaving John without a word, she headed for the front door of her new home. She stepped inside the empty house and took in the old wood floors and white walls. The house was small but had more than enough room for one person.*

*Standing in the middle of the living room, she could easily picture Simon's furniture in the space. She could imagine him sitting on the sofa talking about his day while he lazily ran his hand up and down her leg.*

*She wished playing out that scene brought the kind of comfort she'd found a few months ago, back when he was the anchor in her storm. Back when her storm, which had been so overwhelming, was nothing more than a little thunder. The storm consuming her now was more like a hurricane, and even memories of Simon weren't enough to calm her.*

*This was her life now. This empty house. This foreign place. This quiet.*

*It was the quiet that was going to do her in. No more incessant talking about whatever had drawn Katie's attention. No more begging for story time. No more songs being sung with the wrong words and off-key. No more asking Katie to be quiet for just one minute so Mama could think.*

*No more Katie.*

*Caroline was supposed to keep going. Somehow.*

*She was supposed to make a new life for herself now. At least, that was the speech she'd given herself for the entire six-*

*hour drive from Dayton to St. Louis. Simon had given her a place to stay and a contact to help her find a new job. He'd given her a place to land.*

*All she had to do was find a way to get on her feet. All she had to do was learn how to live without her child.*

*Easing down the bags, Caroline sat on the stairs a few feet inside the front door and fumbled with the latch on the tiny backpack she'd brought with her. When she was able to lift the top, she reached in, hoping she wouldn't find what she was seeking. Part of her still hoped she was trapped in some kind of nightmare and that she'd wake up soon.*

*Unfortunately, her fingers brushed the cool metal of the urn she'd put inside as she'd walked out on her old life, confirming what she already knew. This was no dream. Her little girl was dead. Pulling the urn out, Caroline brushed her thumb across the engraving over and over.*

*She stared at her daughter's name and the date of Katie's death, stuck in some strange limbo of not believing this could possibly be true and knowing she had to accept reality so she could find a way to keep going.*

*The sob that forced itself up her throat echoed around the house.*

*The searing pain in her chest was becoming too familiar. She had been numb for weeks following Katie's death. The doctor had prescribed her sedatives, and she'd been eager to take them. The drugs had kept this pain at a manageable level. Her mind was desensitized enough that she hadn't been able to fully connect with how much she was hurting. That fog was lifting now. That pain was hitting her. Hard. The ache started in*

Caroline's heart and burned through her until she couldn't inhale.

"Excuse me," a gentle voice said.

Caroline jolted as she looked up through her tears at an elderly woman standing in the front door. For a moment, she feared she'd walked into the wrong house.

Then the woman smiled sweetly as she held out a tissue. "You must be Caroline."

Confused, Caroline managed to nod.

The woman came closer, lifting the tissue again. "I'm Genetta Walker from next door. Dr. Miller called. He said you'd be moving in for a spell." Her dark eyes drifted down to the urn in Caroline's hands and her shoulders sagged. "I was so sorry to hear about your little girl, honey. No mother should go through that. I promised Dr. Miller I'd be here if you needed anything."

Caroline didn't respond. She couldn't quite understand what was happening.

"When is your furniture coming?" Genetta asked.

Finally accepting the tissue, Caroline dabbed her nose before asking, "Furniture?"

Genetta tilted her head. "Do you have a bed? A couch?"

Caroline shook her head. "I, um, I left that...with..." She almost said she'd left that with her husband, but she refused to keep giving John that title. John Bowman wasn't worthy of that title any more than he'd been worthy of being Katie's father.

"That's okay." Genetta put a hand on Caroline's shoulder and gently squeezed. "I'll call my church. We'll get you some things. Don't you worry about that. When's the last time you ate?"

*"Um. I don't know... Yesterday, I guess."*

*"Well," Genetta said sweetly. "Let's start by getting something in your stomach."*

*Caroline couldn't recall how, but somehow, she ended up at Genetta Walker's table eating some kind of casserole. While she sat silently at the table, Genetta made several phone calls, whispering into the receiver while constantly glancing at Caroline with sad eyes. Caroline would smile each time, robotically, automatically, without feeling. She was thankful for Genetta's kindness, she was thankful for the food, but part of her wanted to be sitting on those stairs, crying as she hugged Katie's urn.*

*She just wanted to be still. Alone. Surrounded by the pain of her loss.*

*Genetta hadn't allowed that. She'd fed Caroline, walked her to her couch, and urged her to lie down. Then she'd tucked a blanket around her and run down a list of people who were already working to get Caroline some belongings.*

*By the end of the following day, several men had carried in a full-sized bed, a couch, and a kitchen table set. Genetta and several other women unpacked and washed dishes from the church basement. They talked to Caroline carefully. She'd never been so acutely aware of people dancing around basic conversation. No one asked where she came from, why she was moving into a house alone with no belongings. More specifically, no one mentioned the urn Caroline couldn't seem to put down.*

*All the while, Caroline smiled and nodded as if she'd actually heard the conversation being directed at her. She hadn't. She was outside herself by then, watching from so far away that nothing felt real.*

When the house emptied, Caroline still hadn't fully come out of her fog, but she knew the kindness was all due to Simon. She had furniture, new clothes, and food in her fridge because Simon had reached out to his old neighbor, asking her to step in where he couldn't. He'd taken care of Caroline like he'd promised. She wouldn't have survived this if he hadn't helped her. She owed him. She owed him everything. She didn't know if she could ever repay him, but she did know she wouldn't have found a way to carry on if he hadn't intervened.

She turned her attention to the phone Genetta had brought over, wanting to call and thank Simon, but she stopped before grabbing the receiver. If she called him, she'd break down. She'd broken down so many times in the last forty-eight hours. She was free from John. Free from his drinking and the mind games that had kept her off-balance for so long.

But look what it had taken. Look at the price she'd paid.

Shame washed over Caroline, filling every part of her. She'd failed as a mother. She'd failed as a wife. She'd failed as a lover.

Everything she touched, everyone she touched, had paid for her shortcomings.

She owed Simon for helping her, but calling him now would just be extending the pain she'd already caused. He'd feel obligated to continue helping her, to continue checking on her. He'd feel obligated to save her, but he couldn't. Nobody could.

The best way to pay Simon back for his kindness was to leave him alone and let him get on with his life without her.

———

Carol listened to Simon talk about his day as she walked upstairs to Alyssa's guest room. He'd submitted his letter of retirement two days after Christmas and promptly put in vacation time to go to Missouri.

"I woke up to a beautiful sunrise over the mountains," he said as she closed the bedroom door for some privacy. "Then I hiked for about an hour before I even had coffee."

"Oh, that's brave," Carol teased.

"Well, I lose all my inhibitions when I'm here."

Carol laughed as she sat on the bed. "Good to know."

"Why's that? Are you finally going to give in and visit me?"

"Doesn't sound like I can handle this wilder side of you."

Simon chuckled. "I'll rein it in for you."

"I'd appreciate that."

"Just so you know," he said, "if you happened to show up before the tenth of January, the guest room would be ready for you."

Carol smiled as she leaned against the headboard. "No pressure, though."

"Absolutely none. Even when I send you pictures of the amazing view from my deck, there's still no pressure."

With a twinge of jealousy in her gut, she recalled the photos he'd shown her when they'd had dinner in St. Louis. "I'm not feeling pressured at all."

"I want you to know that you're welcome. You don't even have to ask first."

"I do know. Thank you."

"One of these days, you'll take me up on it."

"One of these days," she agreed.

The silence on the other end of the line said so much. She'd disappointed him. All her life, Carol had bent herself into pretzels trying to never disappoint anyone. She'd tried. Rarely succeeded, but she did try. Familiar dread formed a hot ball in her stomach as she waited for the inevitable fallout. "I know you want me to—"

"Caroline," he stated, "what I want is irrelevant. You need to make these decisions for yourself."

"You're probably the only person who feels that way. Everyone wants me to do what makes them feel better."

"I want you to be happy. That's what I want."

"I wish I knew how," she said after a few seconds. "I promised John I wouldn't continue sitting in my office pissing my life away by living the same day over and over. I was in a rut when he found me, and I promised him I would travel because that was what he wanted."

"Is that what you wanted?"

"At the time, that seemed like the answer," she said. "I would have done exactly what he said. I would have gone back to Houston after he died, gone back to work, and lived my life stuck on repeat. Being on the road was supposed to keep me moving forward...somehow." She frowned when she realized how lame her explanation was. No wonder everyone was worried about her. "Now I'm staring this thing down and I'm feeling a little lost, to be honest. I've sold my house, I've given up my career, and now, I'm... Now I'm preparing to slay my demons, and I don't even have a place to call home. I feel like I don't belong anywhere. That's taking its toll."

"Because this didn't suit you. This was a lifestyle that suited John. John was the one who was carefree and reckless, Caroline. You were the grounded one. You're no longer grounded. You're no longer living your life the way you feel comfortable."

"That was kind of the point," she said.

"I'm not trying to psychoanalyze you."

Carol scoffed. "I hope to hell not. We don't have that kind of time."

"I want to help you make sense of things."

Dropping her head back against the headboard, she considered his comment for a few seconds. "You always did. You always tried to get me to see the bigger picture. I was never good at that."

"This isn't some great mystery that can't be solved. Your nature is to be logical. Sensible. Centered. There is absolutely nothing wrong with that. Personally, I find those attributes to be very attractive."

"Oh, I'm glad someone does."

Simon ignored her sarcastic retort and continued. "The problem is that sometimes, you cling to them a little too hard."

"Wait, are you saying my best attributes are also my biggest flaws?"

"The other problem is your mouth. You never stop running it."

Carol rolled her head back as she laughed. "You're not the first person who's said that to me."

"I'm shocked. Really." Though his words were serious, she could hear the teasing in his voice.

"You should hear what people say about my overthinking."

"I can't imagine," Simon stated.

As the lighter moment faded, Carol exhaled loudly. "I've never been good at finding my way on my own."

"Nobody is," Simon softly said. "We all count on friends and family to talk with and hash things out. I think you're trying too hard."

"Me? Try too hard?"

"What does Alyssa say?"

Carol debated if she wanted to share that with him. In the spirit of being more honest with herself and those around her, she closed her eyes before admitting, "She says I should be in Missouri with you."

"I like her. I like her a lot."

Smiling, Carol shook her head. "I'm trying really hard to do right by you this time. However, I'm starting to think you're one of those guys who likes being abused."

"That all depends on who is doing the abusing."

"Oh my God," she moaned but then laughed. "I want to get my head on straight before..."

"Before?" he asked when she didn't finish.

She pressed her lips together as she again debated how much to open herself up. "What are we doing, Simon? What's happening here?"

"What do you think?"

"No," Carol said. "I asked you. We touched on this on Christmas. You were sad, and I'd been drinking. So, I...I need some clarity. What do you want from this? What do you want from me?"

Again, he was quiet. "This feels like a trap."

She quirked a brow. "How so?"

"You've told me more than once you're not ready for more. If I tell you I am, you could use that as a reason to run from me."

Carol swallowed hard. "I guess I could. Or I could use it as a reason to get my shit together so I can feel like I have something to offer someone."

"You have so much to offer someone," he said.

A strange warmth started in her belly and swirled up around her heart. "I had an amazing life with Tobias."

"I know you did."

"I'm scared to let him go. I'm scared that..." She laughed wryly. "I don't even know what I'm scared of. I'm just scared."

"You've been through a lot of changes in the last two years. And you're staring down a lot more. That's scary."

"Sometimes I wish you'd tell me to snap out of it."

He chuckled. "Would that help? Really? Has that ever helped anyone?"

"Probably not." She grabbed the rose quartz worry stone off the nightstand and ran her thumb over the engraving. *No Regrets.* "You know, we used to spend so much time talking about what could be. We're older now. We have to be more realistic about life. I carry a lot of baggage. More than most.

I'm trying to unload some of that, but this isn't going to be easy. I have to get a sense of self before I can be anything to anyone again."

"That's exactly why I'm hesitant to answer your question. You'll overthink it. You'll pick my words apart. You'll find a thousand hidden meanings that aren't really there."

She scoffed. "Well, so you know, I've already picked apart everything you could possibly say to me a thousand times. Might as well ease some of my stress and give me one thing to obsess about instead of a million."

He exhaled audibly. "Okay. Here it is. My girls are both in college now. Pretty soon, I'll be going to graduations and then weddings. Someday, in the not too distant future, I expect to be holding my first grandchild. I would really like someone to share those things with," Simon said. "More than that, Caroline, I'd like that person to be *you*."

Carol's heart skipped a beat. Maybe two. She rarely let herself think about how she'd never be a grandmother, but she was aware. As her circle of friends aged and became grandparents, Carol knew she'd never hold that title. She'd accepted that long ago, but there was a shadow that hung over her. There was a lingering reminder that she didn't have the children or the family she'd always wanted.

She couldn't find the right words to respond. Pressing her hand to mouth, she tried to stop a choked sob from leaving her.

Simon continued, filling the silence between them. "I'd like us to take family vacations to places we'd hate if not for our grandkids having so much fun. When we're not traveling with our family, I'd like us to go hiking in the woods and read by the fire and have all those things we used to talk about. That's what I want. What do you think?" he asked. "Is that too much?"

She opened her mouth, but she'd lost her words. Once again, Simon Miller was offering her the life she'd always dreamed of having. She'd turned her back on him last time because she hadn't wanted to hurt Katie. She had no reason now, other than the fear that made her incapable of answering him.

"Maybe I shouldn't have mentioned stuffy graduations, stressful weddings, and screaming grandkids," he said, as if he were trying to lighten the mood.

"Actually," she managed around the lump that had formed in her chest, "that sounds really nice."

"Which part?"

"All of it," she said. "All of it sounds amazing. I'm terrified I'm going to hurt you, Simon." She bit her lip before asking, "You know I'm a disaster, right? I'm a complete and utter disaster."

"Yes," he said flatly, "but I'd really like you to be my disaster. When you're ready."

Carol swallowed hard and closed her eyes. As soon as she did, images of the life he wanted to share filled her mind. "Soon," she whispered. "I'll be ready soon."

# FOURTEEN

CAROL WATCHED Alyssa lean out her car window and swipe a fob in front of a sensor. Her nerves formed a knot in her stomach as the gate slid open. She'd been here a million times, watched this gate open a million times. The last time she felt this much trepidation was the first time she'd returned to this neighborhood after Tobias's funeral.

"We shouldn't be doing this," Carol said.

"So you've noted." Alyssa eased her car forward. "Repeatedly."

"You shouldn't have that fob."

"You gave it to me."

Carol's eyes widened. "To watch over my house while I was on vacation. Not to...stalk the new owners."

Alyssa snorted. "I haven't stalked anyone. Lately."

Carol shook her head. "Don't expand on that. I don't want to know." Her dread grew as Alyssa crossed into the neighborhood where Carol and Tobias had lived for fifteen years. "Why are we doing this?"

"Because you said last night you wanted to see your house again."

"I was being pathetic after two glasses of wine."

"Never be pathetic with me, Carol. You should know that."

Carol did know. Maybe that's why she'd said it. Alyssa had a way of making things happen. Even when she shouldn't.

Alyssa rolled to a stop sign. Once she turned right, Carol's old house would come into view. She sat at the sign longer than necessary, and Carol understood that the lingering moment was her friend giving her a chance to back out. If she said to turn left, they'd make a loop and head out of the neighborhood.

Carol didn't say anything, so Alyssa turned to the right, and there it was. The home Carol and Tobias had fallen in love with so long ago. The home where they'd tried to have a family, where they'd cried and fought and planned for a future that wasn't meant to be. The brick facade was so familiar yet so strange.

As the car neared the house, Alyssa slowed and then stopped along the curb. Through the fence, Carol could see into the backyard. Tobias's garden remained as vibrant as ever. The new owners hadn't removed it. The relief she felt was unexpected. She hadn't realized how much she'd feared the garden would be gone, but there it was, as lush and vibrant as when he could still tend to the plants every day.

The bushes he'd painstakingly selected for the landscaping in the front remained, as trimmed and well cared for as they'd been when they'd owned the home.

The house was the same. So much so, Carol almost felt as if she hadn't left. Like she was still there. If she walked in through the garage door and into the kitchen, she wouldn't be at all surprised if her decor was on the walls and her furniture sat in the places it had for so long.

Instead of comforting, that feeling was jolting.

She'd left this life months ago. The reason she'd left was because, as John had so bluntly stated, she was stuck in a rut. and she'd stay in that rut until she died or pushed herself out of it. Sitting here and feeling as if she could walk into that house and reclaim her old life, she finally understood what he'd meant. She finally got the point.

This life was gone. She had to let the past go. She had to let Tobias and his garden and all the hopes she'd pinned on him go. Though she already knew this, she could no longer deny that the time to move on had come.

A light breeze blew through the car window. Through the fence, Carol could see the *Salvia dorisana* dancing. A moment later, the fruity scent filled her.

"Okay," she whispered. "I'm listening this time."

"What?" Alyssa asked from the driver's seat.

Carol tore her gaze from her old life and focused on her friend. "I should be sobbing uncontrollably right now."

"Why's that?"

"Because I'm staring at the past, at my life with Tobias. I should be a mess right now."

"Are you doing that stuffing everything into a bottle thing you do?"

Carol shook her head. "No. I'm...okay, Lys." She looked back at the house. "I'm sad, but..."

"You're okay," Alyssa finished.

"That's weird, isn't it?"

"Accepting that life goes on and letting go of soul-crushing pain? No, that's not weird, Carol. That's a healthy part of the grieving process."

"I'm healing," Carol whispered.

"Yeah, babe. You are. You're healing, and that's okay. That's actually really good."

Carol took one last look before blowing her breath out. "Yeah. It is. Let's go."

Alyssa pulled away from the curb.

"Simon has this entire life planned for us," Carol said as they exited through the gate.

"Does it sound awful?"

"No. It sounds perfect." She looked at the familiar bushes and trees that meticulously lined the street. She'd seen the landscaping as a sense of security, that their neighborhood was being taken care of. Now, the perfectly spaced foliage seemed fake, a facade meant to disguise that the real world existed, even inside the perfect neighborhood.

This was a far cry from the woods that surrounded the home Simon had shown her. The wild freedom of trees growing where they pleased was much more appealing than she would have thought. "His kids are both in college," Carol said. "They'll be graduating soon. Simon thinks it's only a matter of time before they're getting married and having kids. He said he wants to share that with me. His kids and grandkids and family vacations. Sounds perfect, right?"

"So why aren't you jumping at it?"

Carol tore her attention from the scenery to look at her friend. "I don't know."

Alyssa kept her eyes on the road but tilted her head in the way she did before dropping some wisdom. "You deserve happiness."

Carol creased her brow. "What?"

"*You deserve to be happy*," Alyssa stated, enunciating each word.

"What if it doesn't work out?" Carol asked. "What if I pin all my hopes on this and he changes his mind, or he falls off a cliff while hiking, or...he slurps his cereal and I have to kill him?"

Alyssa moaned. "Holy shit. This is what keeps you up at night?"

"Those are all very real possibilities. I can't live with a man who slurps."

"There are options. You could wear headphones. Don't buy cereal. Train him how to not slurp."

Carol's smile faded. "What if, six months from now, he realizes he made a mistake?"

"What if, six months from now, he is madly in love with you and making you happier than you ever thought you'd be again?"

"What if his kids hate me?"

"What if they adore you?" Alyssa squeezed Carol's hand. "He's in Missouri right now?"

Carol nodded. "For another week or so."

"How long is the drive? And don't even try to tell me you haven't already checked."

Embarrassed at being caught, warmth rose up her neck. "About eleven hours."

"When we get home, you put your shit in that RV and you go to him."

Carol jerked her head toward Alyssa. "*Go?* Just like that?"

"Just like that," Alyssa stated. "Come on, Carol. Take this chance. You're going to regret it if you don't."

The rose quartz flashed through Carol's mind. She'd rubbed her thumb over the engraving so many times, she felt the bumps without even holding the stone.

*No Regrets.*

"I-I don't think that's a good idea," Carol said. "I mean...I came here for you. I'm here to help you."

"So come back. You said he's there for another week? Go visit him and then come back. I'll still be here, and my life will still be a disaster."

Carol widened her eyes and opened her mouth, searching for a reason she shouldn't go to Simon. A week. She could visit him for a week. She could walk his property and have those long talks that she loved so much.

Alyssa stopped at a red light and turned her face to Carol. "Can you at least admit that you'd like to go?"

Carol nodded. "I want to go."

"So go."

She opened her mouth, waiting for a reason to come out, but her mind was blank. There was no reason she shouldn't go to Simon, except that going to Simon meant she had to actually let go of the past.

———

*Carol jolted at the sound of the alarm from Tobias's phone. The beeping never pulled him from sleep. He would stay blissfully unaware until she reached over and shook him. This morning was no different.*

*"Hey," she mumbled without opening her eyes. "Get up."*

*He slapped his hand onto the phone that rested on the nightstand and snorted. He hadn't even completely woken up, which grated on her nerves. This was their morning routine. For the last twenty years, his alarm went off at five in the morning, but she was the one who woke up. Then she'd spend the next forty-five minutes waking up every time the snooze went off, trying to get Tobias out of bed.*

*She wasn't in the mood this morning, though. She'd been up until almost three working on a presentation she needed to give about a recent drug trial. Very rarely did she let these things shake her, but for some reason she was dreading standing in front of her peers this time. She didn't feel prepared. She hadn't been able to stay focused on the research. Now she was going to show up exhausted.*

*The last thing she wanted was their daily alarm clock battle.*

*"Tobias," she snapped. "Turn that off and get up."*

*He shifted, slowly stirring from sleep, so she rolled onto her side and pulled the covers over her head. She managed to shut out the noise of him getting ready until he climbed onto the bed and leaned over her.*

*"You coming?" he asked.*

*"No."*

*"Why not?"*

*Exhaling, she did her best not to bark at him again. He wasn't the reason she hadn't slept well. There was something off, something she couldn't work through that had her feeling off-balance the last few days. This lecture she had to give shouldn't have had her so out of sorts, but she just couldn't grasp the reports. "I need more sleep before my presentation."*

*"Come on, babe," Tobias coaxed, rubbing his hand over her back. "Running clears your head."*

*"Go," she said, holding the blankets firmly in place when he tried to tug them free. "Get me up when you get back. With coffee," she added.*

*Tobias kissed her head through the blanket and then swatted her ass. "Lazy bum."*

*"Coffee," she reiterated as the bed shifted. Moments later, she was alone, drifting back to sleep.*

*She didn't know how long she'd slept, but the sound of her phone ringing pulled her back to reality. Grabbing for her cell, she cleared her throat and squinted at the clock. Barely after six thirty. She glanced around the room, looking for signs that Tobias had returned from his run. He should have woken her by now.*

*Though she cleared her throat as she connected the call, Carol sounded groggy. "Hello?"*

"Mrs. Denman?" a stranger asked.

And just like that, Carol's world spiraled out of control. Within minutes, she was out of bed, pulling on whatever clothes she'd snagged from the dresser and running for the door. The reason played on a loop in her mind.

Tobias had been hurt. He was at the hospital. She needed to get there as soon as possible.

As Carol rushed to get to his side, she became hyperaware—every light, every sound, every movement amplified. She was beyond alert. She was almost outside her body, experiencing every second in some omniscient view as she sped down the highway and rushed into the hospital.

She jogged to the receptionist sitting behind a long, built-in wooden desk. "I got a call that my husband is here. Tobias Denman."

The woman pecked away on her computer and then turned to a nurse behind her, relaying who Carol was. The woman nodded and then disappeared. Once she was gone, the receptionist suggested Carol have a seat until someone could speak to her.

Carol's heart sank to the depths of her stomach. Her mind flashed back to standing in an emergency room in Dayton as she and John waited for news about Katie. The moment she'd seen the doctor's face, she'd known. Before he even said a word, before he could escort them someplace private to share the news, Carol had known that Katie was gone.

Nausea rolled through her. Putting her hand to her mouth, Carol controlled the urge to be sick as tears filled her eyes. "Is he..."

"No," the receptionist was quick to answer. "I don't know his condition, but he's alive."

That wasn't much comfort, but Carol clung to the words as she nodded. "Okay."

"Please. Have a seat."

Carol glanced behind her at the row of chairs. Clutching her phone to her chest, she debated if she should call Mary. But what would she tell her? Carol didn't know anything yet. Mary would want to know what happened, what his injuries were, if he was going to be okay. Carol couldn't answer any of those. She didn't know.

Maybe he'd had a heart attack. Oh, God. He'd had a heart attack while running and she hadn't been there. She'd been sleeping. Why hadn't she gotten up?

Because she had a presentation. That was why.

Oh, shit. She had a presentation in just a few hours.

Texting her administrative assistant, she let Tiana know Tobias had been in an accident and was at the hospital. She didn't know more than that but didn't think she'd be in today.

Please reschedule the meeting to next week if possible, she typed.

No matter what had happened to Tobias, Carol would surely be back in the office by next week.

"Mrs. Denman?"

She lifted her head, and her heart dropped again. The look in the doctor's eyes... Oh, no. She knew that look.

"I'm Dr. Ameer. I've been treating your husband." The short, dark-haired woman peered around her. "Are you alone?"

"Yes."

"Mrs. Denman..." Her mouth twitched as she debated what to say next. "I think you should call someone."

"Where's my husband?" Carol's voice came out so weak, she barely heard the words herself.

The doctor didn't answer. The pity on her face, the sorrow in her eyes...

Oh, God. Oh, no.

"Is he...alive?" she croaked out.

"Yes." Her voice wasn't any more reassuring than her sympathetic eyes or subdued body language.

"But?" Carol forced herself to ask.

"I don't want to scare you," the doctor said gently.

"But?" she pressed.

She held Carol's gaze. "Your husband was hit by a truck from behind."

Hit? By a truck? The words were foreign, and she had a hard time making sense of them. She was tempted to argue because that was absurd. Illogical.

"The damage is extensive," Dr. Ameer said, as if discussing the vehicle rather than Tobias.

No. No. This didn't make any sense.

"There's no way to prepare you for this," the doctor continued. "His skull was fractured, and his upper back was broken."

Those words she heard. Those words she understood. But she couldn't find the words to respond.

"The next few hours will tell us much more." The doctor's voice faded after that.

Carol couldn't breathe. Her chest was too tight. Her throat

*was too dry. Her heart pounded too hard. She closed her eyes, and though she hadn't prayed in as long as she could remember, she sent a silent plea for her husband to recover.*

*Maybe the doctor was confused. Maybe she was talking to the wrong wife about the wrong husband. Tobias wasn't lying in a bed. He wasn't shattered and fractured. Carol wanted to verify Dr. Ameer had the right patient, but she couldn't find her voice.*

*"Mrs. Denman." Dr. Ameer's tone implied that she'd said her name more than once before Carol focused on her eyes again. "I want you to prepare yourself before you see him."*

*Carol swallowed. "I...um...I used to be a nurse, so..."*

*"It's different when the patient is someone you care about."*

*She bit her lip as, once again, she thought of Katie. In her mind, Carol clearly saw the sterile room where she'd last held her daughter. This wouldn't be like that. This wouldn't be like Katie. This couldn't be like Katie.*

*"I know," Carol managed to whisper.*

*"He's bandaged and on a ventilator," Dr. Ameer said. "There's swelling and bruising on his face. He's not going to look like himself. If you'd like us to call someone to be here with you—"*

*She shook her head abruptly. "No. Please. Take me to him."*

*Dr. Ameer was clearly hesitant. "Okay," she finally said. She turned, and Carol followed her down a hall. The chemical smell made her stomach churn. The sound of machines beeping rhythmically echoed through her head. Every step she took was a step toward a future she didn't want.*

*"He's here." Dr. Ameer gestured toward a closed door. "Come to the nurses' station if you need anything."*

*Carol nodded and then pushed the door to his room open. The moment she stepped inside, she knew her prayer wouldn't be answered. The moment she saw him, she knew.*

*From the first time they'd met, his soul had reached out to hers. The brightness within him illuminated the darkness that surrounded her. That connection was gone now. The tie that had always bound them was broken.*

*Tobias's body was there, but his light was gone.*

———

The dread and anxiety Carol had been feeling all day magnified the moment the rural town where Simon lived came into view. She had opted not to let him know she was on her way to Missouri in case she made it all the way to his driveway and then chickened out. She didn't even make it to his driveway. She made it to a little gas station, where she parked out of the way of other patrons. She sat, staring out at the street, wondering if she could live here.

The community was clean, nestled in the Ozarks, away from the noise of the cities where she'd always lived. Life here would definitely be slower. That was oddly comforting. They could travel whenever they wanted. If she got the urge to immerse herself back in the hustle and bustle, they could take a trip somewhere. Simon had told her he wanted to travel after retiring.

They could go anywhere. See anything. When they were ready, they could return to the quiet seclusion of his mountain home, where they would go hiking and explore the wilderness. They could have the best of both worlds. Together. They'd have everything *together*.

So what the hell was she waiting for?

Carol reached for the key to start the ignition, but instead of turning the key, she pulled it free. Before she took the last stretch of this journey, the last few miles to Simon, she needed a minute or two. She had to be absolutely certain before she walked into his house that she wanted to be there. She was confident now that he wouldn't change his mind, but she had to be certain she wouldn't change hers out of guilt or fear or some foolish need to cling to the past.

After climbing from her seat, she walked into the RV's kitchenette. She came face-to-face with the photo of Tobias and her that she'd put on the fridge the day they'd bought the vehicle. The love they'd shared was evident in the photo. Carol traced his face with her fingertips, and a million memories came rushing forward. From the first time they'd kissed to the intimate moments on their wedding day, all the tears and fights and laughs they'd shared over the years came to the surface at once.

Carol's lips trembled, but she blinked the tears away before they could fall. "I'll always love you," she whispered to his image. "Forever." Sliding the magnet off the photo, she took the image from the fridge and held it for several long minutes before taking it to the RV's bedroom. Pulling open the built-in nightstand's drawer, she added the photo to the others she kept there. As she sank onto the bed, she looked at the bands hugging her left ring finger. The diamond sparkled like brand new. She'd never imagined she'd ever remove the symbol of their marriage, but as she watched the light dance off the gem, she knew she had to.

She could not walk into Simon's life until she'd let go of the life she'd shared with Tobias. She could not look into the future until she'd let go of the past. Tobias would be a part of her forever. He would always be in her heart. She would never forget him. But she couldn't cling to him with one hand and reach for Simon with the other.

Holding her breath, Carol slid the rings from her finger and set them on top of the photos. She stared at the rings for what seemed like hours before easing the drawer shut. Lifting her left hand, she considered how foreign it looked without the rings that had been there for so long. Though she'd never had much of a tan since she tended to burn, the skin beneath was paler than the rest. In no time at all, the color would balance. The reminder that her rings were gone would fade.

Pushing herself up, Carol walked back to the fridge and yanked the door open. She frowned as she stared at the empty compartment. She'd cleaned out her fridge when she'd arrived at Alyssa's house. She hadn't planned to be on the road again for weeks, maybe even months. In her rush to get on the road before too late in the day, she hadn't put anything back in.

Peering out the window at the little store, she debated how much her sudden need for a drink was thirst and how much was procrastination. In the end, that didn't matter, because she climbed from the RV and headed inside.

Bright signs hung over the refrigerators that lined the

back wall. Beer. Snacks. Drinks. She headed for the cold drinks. Standing in front of the glass door that held a variety of bottles, she weighed her options—for too long. She was standing there far too long. This wasn't that hard of a decision. Plain water or flavored water. A sports drink. Tea.

She'd had this same type of indecision when she'd been standing at a store in Arizona, debating which water shoes to buy. That had only been a few months ago, but somehow, it seemed like a lifetime had passed. In those months, she'd faced more fears than she thought possible.

Digging into her pocket, she wrapped her fingers around the worry stone and thought of Harold. If he were standing beside her, she had no doubt he'd be offering words of wisdom about making choices based on what was best for her now—not based on traumas of the past or fears of the future, but now.

She had to make her choice based on what was best for her now.

Pick one.

Stay or go.

*Just choose.*

"The suspense is killing me," someone said from several feet away.

Carol closed her eyes. Simon had said those exact words to her years ago. Turning her head to him as she'd done so long ago, she found him watching her. The serene smile on his face melted her heart, as it had always done.

"Are you going to buy a drink or not?" he asked.

She saw in his eyes that he was fully aware her debate wasn't about the refreshments. He knew her better than that.

"This is a very important decision," she said quietly.

"I can tell," he responded as he closed the distance between them. "Should we discuss the pros and cons of each?"

Carol tilted her head, pondering. "Well," she said, "if I buy a drink, I'm committed to drinking the drink. I'm not sure if I'm ready for that."

"Nothing is ever final," Simon told her. "You could decide you don't want the drink and throw it away."

"I could. But after standing here all this time trying to decide what I want, throwing it away would just feel wasteful. Don't you think?"

"Well, you could buy the drink, take the drink home, put it on ice, and see how you feel about it later."

She creased her brow. "What if I wait too long?"

"The drink will still be there," he said. Gripping her left hand, he looked at her finger as he brushed his thumb over where her rings had been. "It's okay if you're not sure. We have time."

She hesitated. He couldn't know that. Nobody knew how much time they had. That was a lesson Carol had learned far too many times in her life. But the longer she waited, sitting in uncertainty, the less time they would have.

Seeing uncertainty in his gaze, she realized he was probably having the same concerns that she'd been voicing. She could change her mind as easily as he could. She could walk away. She'd done it before. But she wouldn't this time.

Looking into his eyes, she knew she wouldn't walk away again.

Finally, she nodded one slow, resolute nod. "I'm sure."

Simon pulled her into his arms and hugged her close. Carol burrowed deeper into his embrace, snuggling even closer as he cupped the back of her head.

"I'm so glad you're here," he whispered into her ear.

Closing her eyes tightly, she held her breath for a few seconds. When she leaned back, she offered him a soft smile. "So am I, but, Simon, I'm just starting to heal. I'm going to need a little patience."

"I'm a doctor," he stated. "I have lots of *patients*."

Carol frowned when his lips twitched. "Did you just make a joke?"

Simon started to laugh but forced the grin from his face. "Yes. It was terrible. I'm sorry."

She started to pull back, but he didn't release her. "I'm baring my soul to you in a convenience store, and you're making corny jokes." Though she was trying to chastise him, she couldn't help the smile tugging at her lips as well.

He cleared his throat. "I sincerely apologize. You were saying?"

"I'm going to need patience because I'm not done healing," she said. "I want to be clear about that."

Simon stroked her hair from her face. "You've been clear. Now let me be clear. No relationship is ever easy. We'll have ups and downs, but I won't give up. Not after all this time."

"I want to be here with you, but that doesn't mean I won't continue to hurt for Tobias."

"I know you love Tobias," Simon whispered. "I'm not asking you to stop loving him. I'm just asking you to consider that maybe you could love me too."

Resting her hand on his cheek, she looked into his light brown eyes and gave voice to a truth she'd been wrestling with for months. "I've always loved you, Simon. We just didn't happen at the right time."

His lips curved into a soft smile. "What about now?"

Carol smiled too. "Now is good."

# EPILOGUE

*Five years later*

CAROL STARED out as the sun peeked over the horizon. The light brightened by the minute, illuminating the shadows cast by the mountains. Fog had settled among the trees in the valley below, creating a dreamlike vision that spread out for miles before her.

The birds woke, chirping to let the world know they'd survived the night. Tugging a blanket around her as she sipped her coffee, she embraced the peace of the moment. Just like the sun finding a way through the fog to the trees below, peace had found its way to Carol's heart and mind.

The serenity was no longer just in the woods around her but had finally made its way into her soul.

She thought of Katie and Tobias often—she even thought of John from time to time—but memories of them no longer brought her to her knees. She could think back, smile, and be thankful for the time they'd shared. The holes they'd left in her heart could never be filled, but they no longer had the ability to throw her life into disarray.

Carol had learned to see her time with them as a blessing rather than seeing her life without them as a tragedy. That hadn't been an easy transition but one that had put her on the road to healing, one that she likely wouldn't have been able to stay on if she hadn't had Simon there to support her.

When he'd first come into her life, he'd brought a sense of calm with him. For a long time, she'd chalked that up to how chaotic her life had been, but even now, all these years later, he had the ability to soothe her simply by being. A smile, a touch, the sound of his voice—those things were like an elixir for all that ailed her heart, mind, and soul.

Tobias had once said that the universe had bigger plans than Carol might know about. She had a hard time believing she had to go through so much hurt to get to this point, but she couldn't deny that she was destined to be here. With Simon. With their family.

As if he'd read her thoughts, the door opened and Simon emerged. Carol's smile spread.

"There she is," Simon said to the toddler in his arms. "There's Grandma."

Carol lifted her arms, and the little girl leaned toward her. Tucking Adele into the blanket with her, Carol kissed her granddaughter's head. The scent of strawberry shampoo lingered in the curls. The scent reminded Carol of Katie. However, instead of feeling hollow inside, Carol pulled Adele closer. Hugged her tighter. Kissed her one more time.

As always, Simon could sense when Katie crept into Carol's thoughts. He reached out, waiting for her to put her hand in his. As soon as she did, he brushed his thumb over the wedding ring he'd put there three years prior and kissed the gold band.

"Why are you up so early?" Carol asked.

"She came in looking for you," Simon explained as he sat in the seat next to her. "One of these days, she'll come in looking for Grandpa."

Carol chuckled. "I don't think so. She's Grandma's girl. Aren't you, babe?" After kissing the little one's head, she asked Simon, "Everyone else is still sleeping, then?"

"As far as I can tell." He settled in and looked out at the rising sun. "How do you feel about pancakes and bacon?"

"Are you cooking?" she asked with a smirk.

"I guess."

"Then I'm all for it."

Simon smiled too. "If I cook, you have to clean up."

Carol considered his offer before rolling her head to look at him. "The diner opens at seven."

Simon laughed. "Yeah. It does."

They frequented the small restaurant in town more often lately since neither was in the mood to cook or clean up, but Carol didn't mind. The people were nice, the food was good, and leaving a tip was easier than doing dishes. Besides, when they had family visiting, their time was better spent hiking and sightseeing. Carol didn't care to go to the nearby lake, but she didn't have the fear she'd initially had when their guests wanted to go swimming. While she would never be comfortable playing in the water, she understood others didn't share her fears. She also understood that she couldn't expect them to avoid the lake to appease her as Tobias had avoided rafting.

"Birdie," Adele said, pointing into the distance.

A flock of birds flew from the trees below. Carol's breath caught as she recalled another time she'd witnessed a scene like that—she and John had been in Yellowstone, spreading Katie's ashes. They'd finally made peace with each other and the loss of their daughter. Seeing the flock now, with her husband holding her hand and their first grandchild sitting in her lap, nearly brought tears to Carol's eyes.

Whenever she saw a beam of sunlight, she knew Tobias was shining down on her. And whenever she saw a flock of birds, she'd swear Katie was smiling from Heaven.

"Everything okay?" Simon asked, tugging lightly at her hand.

Carol rested her cheek against Adele's head as she smiled at him. "Everything is perfect. Absolutely perfect."

THE END

## ACKNOWLEDGMENTS

Several medical professionals assisted with various parts of this book:

Many thanks to Aubrey Cutchin and Lacy Jones for their medical and emotional insights when dealing with the loss of a loved one.

Thank you, Dr. Melinda Pheanis Preston, for taking time to help me better understand online counseling and PTSD.

Your contributions to Carol's journey were greatly appreciated.

ALSO BY MARCI BOLDEN

A Life Without Water Series:

A Life Without Water

A Life Without Flowers

A Life Without Regrets

Stonehill Series:

The Road Leads Back

Friends Without Benefits

The Forgotten Path

Jessica's Wish

This Old Cafe

Forever Yours

The Women of Hearts Series:

Hidden Hearts

Burning Hearts

Stolen Hearts

Secret Hearts